Letter.

Thank you both
so much for letting
me write this Sunday.

Etched in Stone

The First Fountain of Fortitude

(Unlimited Version)

& hope
the books
are more appreciated
than my music.

Robert J. Koyich

Lots & lots of love,
luck, life, & joy
to you. Thank you
for being primary people
in my life. /Robert

ISBN-10: 1984107690
ISBN-13: 978-1984107695

DEDICATION

To the facts of the pacts made that let us wade amongst the sunsets.
Though the pets hold the fold of the elective enrolled, the Jets own the
mould of life as an elective we enrolled.

CONTENTS

The Third Round   1

With Thanksgiving   7

Hold the Bond   17

Chart a Course   25

Siamo Internazionale   33

I'm Impatient   41

A Shard of Misdirection   49

In Faith of Our Truth   57

Plotting and Planning   65

Another Row of Seed   73

Choices of Time   81

Choices of Truth   89

Acknowledgments   97

About the Author   99

THE THIRD ROUND

I don't think people yet understand or appreciate the puzzle I've found myself in. There are very opposite and divergent layers of disparity in my awareness just before starting to write this book.

My position in life sees between the layers of status and income; there are forces of those near entirely without, and some that are barely getting by. Some have a home, a job, and in some cases a car or truck, yet there also are some with an abundance of income contrasting those with near nothing.

Regarding income, I know that I have less than many people who have a job. I also understand I am blessed and have access to more than some other people. Some people cannot receive PWD (a disability income) or even welfare and need support. There also are others that work *and* also receive governmental benefits.

The people that have jobs and an income of $24,000 a year are earning more than I had in 2016 and 2017. For those that made more, I wish you can create and acquire even more ethically and allow some for those that want improved lives and situations. When we have money, we can make a more significant impact depending on how we use it.

I don't work a regular hourly paid job. I do, though, put in a fair deal of effort and work. Some would laugh at the idea that writing can be a viable career or profession, or that it's work, yet much is required to bring books into the world. Many levels of skill, commitment, and devotion are needed to form a book, and I *have* chosen to work with the creative pathway.

As of April 2018, I'd not yet earned much money from writing, yet I deem the role and function of authorship potentially quite valuable beyond earnings. There are intrinsic gains of self-awareness and sharing lessons that may help others. For those that write, I hope you find the benefits and increases in your work too.

Some may wonder why I don't have to work a job like they have to. I agree that PWD is for people that can't function at work, and I am a person in that situation. Some people on PWD contribute in different ways, and even when unable to work full-time, there is value in human connection and being a contact in the community.

I know from past jobs and experiences that I'm not capable of working as a full-time employee. My near-violent reactions by being held or trapped in work positions are not a benefit for anyone. I had lost my sanity and composure when I worked as a dishwasher, freaked out at customers when I worked at Wendy's, and I couldn't tolerate some behaviours and spiritual energies when I worked graveyards at a gas station.

Regarding my life, I've sometimes found myself barely able to cope with being alive, let alone being responsible enough to be employed. When I was writing *Fields of Formation,* I was pushed far to the edges of safety and sanity. I'm incredibly thankful and fortunate to be alive. It may not seem it, yet my life has been difficult at times.

I have what I have, yet some aggravation from others may exist. It may be because I have grace and blessings that they don't and also because I don't work a job I hate as some do. My thankfulness may not be entirely understood or appreciated, and though I may not have much income, I'm grateful for what I have.

I've often had a concern about what others think. With the

extreme disparity between myself having a home, food, and water compared to those that don't, it makes me want to help balance out. I choose to provide for others, though my work hasn't yet earned myself a primary living income for myself, let alone providing for people in our community.

I've attempted a creative income through authorship and music, and by using the sales of books and music as a pathway to earnings, my efforts and merits shall hopefully result in a win/win. If I can share my work and earn money by selling books, maybe I can be accepted as a contributor to our society.

Shifting to personal relations and people we know, many would like to be our friends and not just contacts or customers. Of Gary Vaynerchuk's statement "marketers ruin everything," how shall we find a balance of engagement and genuine care coupled with the ability to earn prosperity?

By now, the people that like me as a person, and don't want to read what I've formed, may be put off by me marketing to earn sales. If I establish a livable income from my work though, it's also a fact I've not marketed well up to this point. I have spammed some people with my books, and the idea of Providing Point, my charitable work and cause, is asking for money too.

The big hairy audacious goal of Providing Point is to provide food, shelter, and water for *all* people. To the people in the town I live in, it seems like a completely irrational goal, yet I understand the models for future growth and how we can share if we have more than others.

It is a humanitarian viewpoint to believe that people should have their own basic needs met, and perchance prosperity had denied me from a guilty conscience. I love my life, and I wish others adore theirs too, yet it seems something is not right.

An additional difficulty I find myself in is that it doesn't matter what I want, it's what others want. If others want to be negatively irenic and aim at me for being too ambitious, then why is it okay for others to have materialistic or other grand wants?

If my desire is basic human decency, safety, and a solution

for many through shared responsibility, how can I achieve that on my own? I could get angry to vent and purge all my negative angst because it seems I'm going nowhere, or I could encourage another to delve into my theories and ideas for a more cohesive unity.

Even if I can propose a solution and articulate it for another to hear or read, what would it matter if no one else understands, listens to, or supports it? I see the distribution of my books as seeds that can be shared and planted in people's gardens. It starts at home, yet so few have shown any interest in my books. The books provide awareness and new thought, yet I know I can't force people to read or care; it has to be an open invitation.

If ideas and ethical recommendations encourage others to share and foster positive reciprocation, then is that not an additional layer of good? Dare we find our understanding is a conduit for the benefit of many in multiple ways also? How shall we advance this work for a more prosperous future for others and not only myself?

I need to set myself aside and work for others again. If the seeds we sow germinate, they shall sprout and grow in the future gardens and fields, though how shall we use the yields? I revert the idea in upon itself again. I remind myself that it's my responsibility to sow, develop, and tend the soil.

If these ideas and creations are the seeds I believe them to be, then I must trust that others will use them. Some may never fully flourish, yet I think it's worth planting ideas to grow some fantastic things and prepare for harvest. Perchance it is a law of numbers thing again; plant more seeds, and more shall grow. How shall we use the yields? That's part of the magic.

I fear a penance and retaliation for not pushing strongly enough for pledges or the sales of the books. If the objective is to provide for people, then why have I not pushed more vigorously for patrons or sales? If we develop ethical marketing skills and don't abuse awareness, then shall we achieve some fantastic results?

The intent, purpose, and function of the books have shifted

a lot since the first book, *Finding Natalie*. The obsessive path of wishing to share my textbook cliché wishes and whims also shows my ideas strafe me away from conflict. I am a solitary person focusing on the computer and using the digital landscape is the way I share my thoughts with other people.

I sometimes dislike hearing myself speak, and even if not tot the same people, I repeat myself a lot. When I write, I can form elaborate ideas and thoughts, and it's a lot easier to read them instead of hearing myself chatter on and on. Some of the ideas that come out of my face add that a book is permanent compared to a conversation.

A massive bonus to writing a book is when the mind and thoughts go on cycling, tripping up, and dissecting time; writers can share one coherent linear view and sequence. An author's thinking can weld insecurities without interruption as one domino topples into a series of the written word.

We can give a chance to carry on and forward with the process without having to react telepathic assailants, and use a delicate dance of boundaries and ethics that challenge us to participate. When some people are crucially inceptive, there can be a dance instead of a fight.

As humans, though, we may be invasive of offensive without even knowing it. A person may be put into an uncomfortable or defensive position, and not by a physical threat, yet instead by a reactive nature that might instinctively lash out or scrabble for self-preservation. I have my shortcomings and faults, and I also know when someone pressures or attempts to coerce me into doing things, I have become reluctant.

These books are where other people and I seem to understand I still need to learn many lessons. The conclusions of another may shift the attitude and actions of allowing another person their autonomy. Space to make our own choices and decisions often finds the correct results naturally follow; especially when we have proper ethical knowledge.

I don't always know what is right and accurate. When I find errors in my thoughts, actions, or text, I must become aware.

I acknowledge some mistakes, and I also must accept my transgressions. My secular repentance holds a dangerous edge; I can write and process some of my faults openly, though I hope that doing so is not my hubris.

Admitting mistakes may be a stepping stone to atoning and adjusting behaviours, yet this maybe is where I should speak up more often. When there are mistakes, and others know how we feel when we're shifting paths, we can still make bad choices. When we are wrong and repent, we can always change our efforts and develop forgiveness.

What do I hope for you? First, I should know who 'you' are. As these books have formed, I have sometimes written to specific individuals, yet the pronoun 'you' can be used as a general outwards inclusive word.

It's also true that when we capitalize the Y as You, that a religious context can bring God into the meld. I've mentioned that in previous books, yet you may not have read them, and the premise is relevant.

A value that I hold is *inclusion* as it's a word of unity. For those who've not encountered me and my writing, then I should mention some of the base bridging principles and ideas that I use. PLUR is a primary one from raver culture that signifies peace, love, unity, and respect.

We can't yet know what will have happened with the results of the books, and I can't always tell you when they'll be complete. I can, though, wish we reach the three-part book called *Shards of my Soul* that holds *Etched in Stone* as the first section.

Building towards the future, we learn bit by bit. We gather, hone, and meld the shards. There is a lot of work to be done, though if we process and move one grain of sand at a time, step by step, we shall see the future when we get there.

WITH THANKSGIVING

I'm kind of glad that I think my life is like a soap opera sometimes. I prefer that far more than it being an action or horror film. I have a concern about organized crime and plots and plans aimed at me sometimes, yet there is a lot of care and love for some characters in the drama.

Cued from the keyword 'drama' I also hope and wish that my life not be a tragedy; I'm not a tragic hero. I thought of learning what the word hubris meant in class the other day; an excessive pride or self-confidence. I have had a concern that I'm often near a fatal flaw, yet this is where cleaning some of my innards and bringing some faults to light to shed them away may be helpful. Part of my journey and process is to clean up my behaviours and thoughts.

It was Friday of the 2017 Thanksgiving weekend when I started this chapter. I was inclined to write a chapter about what I'm grateful for and note a Lewis Howes webinar this past week reminded me something; to live in gratitude.

I *am* exceptionally thankful that I am alive, and I have works to form. I carry ideas and my foolish faith and belief that some good will come to Earth through me writing and recording. I also am dearly glad that *The Sands of Yesterday* formed and that the primary commitments and ideas for the Seed Fund and Providing Point formed in the previous three books.

I should not build a house on sand, yet remind us that sedimentary stone is a thing that may become metamorphic. I'd like to use this book not just as a declaration of my wishes and hopes, though also to show the transformation. The saying of 'water under the bridge' means to say that the debris from above is carried down the river to return to the ocean.

We should not forget about how we send thoughts out the world and that we act this way. The artwork for *The Sands of Yesterday* has a photo of an ocean shore, yet there might be far much more for us to explore. I wonder if to write a section about a coral reef and the metaphors of sharks, pirates, and scuba diving.

I practice carrying gladness and thankfulness and also open up parts of myself that I may not like, yet want to understand. I use my writing as self-help and healing as, up to now, I still don't have an actual therapist; a great and good thing for people to have.

When I formed this, I also was without a direct mentor, though the people online and their lessons guide me. Through their experience and lessons, some online people have shared and taught me so much for free. People like me who haven't had money for their products and services must remind them their work still has a substantial positive effect. I thank them each for their generosity of love, knowledge, blessings, and wisdom.

I found myself thinking of Gabby Bernstein, and her book *The Universe Has Your Back*. I recommended the book to those that are searching for clarity and understanding. I first suggested the book to a friend nicknamed Emerald Sprite. Emerald is a dear, kind, bright, and bubbly friend, and I want her to find the profound spiritual lessons Gabby shares.

Gabby's sign is an owl, so I bought a stuffy owl to relay to Emerald. She passed on it, so instead, I gave the owl to Opal Sprite, a different rad and super-kind friend, as a gift. Some of the lovestones (gals that are loved) have been so incredibly kind and welcoming to me. They are dearly appreciated and valued for their compassionate treatment of myself.

I'm also thankful for the two leading card shops in town. Both shops have let me sort cards for credit and are places where some pretty rad people gather. The earnings from sorting help me a lot with my no money/no magic boundary, and I value the friendships and contacts made at the shops.

I had run myself into bankruptcy in 2015 by spending extravagantly on Magic cards with a line of credit. Even though if I had kept my collection I would have a substantial amount of high-value cards; I had sold them. The cards were a significant investment worth far more than when I sold them, though buying Magic cards was an addiction. We know that any form of excessive spending with imaginary money is not always a good idea.

I feel kind of sad that I've not acknowledged my parents and family yet. Adjectives would cheapen how appreciative I am for my parents, yet I'm also happy that my cousin has backed off and given me space to live my own life. I appreciate family and know that I've not reached out to some cousins too much. They may or may not feel the neglect.

Regarding my cousin Alex, he signed onto Patreon as the first Providing Point patron with a $5/month pledge! My extended family (non-blood) have some crucial links in my life recently with conversations, yet we've not met in the past three to four years.

I've sometimes felt sad about forgetting or neglecting people. That can be spun to a positive too, though. If I feel bad that I've overlooked or ignored some, I also remember that those people do matter to me and that I care about them. Sometimes it is best to let others live their lives without jumping into their worlds.

The ability to invert our awareness and think on the opposite sides of a polar idea can be helpful. If we think of having lack of something, we also can think of the gladness we have of that thing because it's something we had. We can even be thankful we may find some of those things or people return to our lives in the future.

I feel relieved that my developing awareness and ability shift and stay on positive notes, waves, and energy more recently. When I become aware of adverse or invasive tendencies, when something or someone is terrible for me, shifting to authentic goodness can be a positive habit.

It's pretty cool to be able to acknowledge bad things and source positive behaviours from our awareness. In *From the Valley to the Fountain*, I talked about smoking and how I gain some benefits from tobacco. I learn some vital truths and pleasure from cigarettes, though I note they're not something I would ever recommend.

Truth is a thing, and though reality's not always bright sunshine, Emerald Sprite commented about how she's seen people are becoming far more accepting of others and not so much trying to control other's behaviours.

Control can be a positive thing, though. I like and value self-control, and as I evolve to be less judgmental and more supportive, I also must not condone some things. Acceptance and forgiveness of ourselves and others is a fantastic idea and can lead to grace, for when we can accept life and learn to appreciate and acknowledge our actual merits too, we can both prune our faults and bolster our positive qualities.

I like and love that I've seen the value some people hold by working and having jobs. Some people have earned trips and vacations, they have been able to buy things that they want, and some also have had the luxuries they enjoy such as meals at restaurants and vehicles. People have these things because they've found a source that will pay them an income.

When I talk about Providing Point ideas, some say they also like the idea, though few have signed up. The few that have want to help others, and I'm appreciative of their generosity. I see generosity with my books too as some have given me money for books even when they know I might have shared a copy for free. Some people want to support others and decline free things.

Many people that I've offered books have said 'no' too. I am entirely okay with 'no' when I offer a book to someone. If they don't want to read it, they don't like me, or they honestly have any other reason not to read a book, I've learned to be okay with just that. As some mentors tell us that asking people is okay, the ability to be okay with a 'no' is also an exceptionally vital ability.

I'm thankful I have my basic needs met. I'm glad I have a home, food, and water and I'm fortunate to have a computer. I'm pleased to have a bus pass, that I can go to school, and that I can go to Toastmasters. I'm grateful I can attend church, that I have books to read and share, and that we seed many of the ideas for a combined Freedom Solution.

My attitudes have shifted a lot in the past couple years towards a more positive understanding. I remind myself that I've had enough resources to cover smokes, my bills, and even coffee and tea. I've not needed to buy furniture or a washer or dryer in the past couple of years, and I have enough cutlery, dishes, and shelf and storage space. My printer works, and I've had backup cartridges of ink and paper. I've even had blank CDs from a dear friend so that I can share my music with people for free!

I'm also sometimes baffled as to why I'm allowed to live in a first world country! Although some people complain about the government, I'm a person that values the systems and services that the Canadian and provincial government have in place that allow me to live the life I live. I may not be above the poverty line according to national or provincial standards, though my life is so incredibly rich in so many different ways.

I'm also so very fortunate to have learned some ethical ideals vital to my wellbeing. I too must assist others with their lives even if I meekly wish not to push so actively to some. I am thankful to have what I have, yet it can't all be only for my benefit.

Some online mentors tell us that if we earn more, then we can share more; I like and value that idea. I know as my earnings increase I can do far more for others, my family, my friends, and myself. There is a wealth of time that I'm thankful for that I'm learning how to manage. If I work to assist, I keep open and accepting, and I strengthen gratitude, it'll be radical. ·

I'm grateful for what I have and am okay to share and give more as the future arrives. I do have materialistic wants, though I see how we can use things and money as a channel to provide for more than ourselves. Two examples? If I have a car, I can deliver people to laces and connect friends to future locations. Two, since 51% of the earnings from book sales go to providing for others, selling books will mean more money for others through Providing Point.

It's clear you've given monetary value if you bought the book, though the additional benefit gives to the planet, community, and people that help with this. You have allowed me to become who I am. I have the chance and opportunity to experience all sorts of life and have been granted life to put on a page. Our work allows us to gather seeds formed throughout the preparation of *Etched in Stone*.

If I get money aware again, I think of how so many other people work to provide so much for the people that cannot. Some people believe in welfare, PWD, and basic living income, and at the point of June 2018, the people who pay taxes and have bought these books have helped with providing for those in need too. Thank you!

I value creativity and artistic seeds in life, and I like the idea of painting groups. A friend named Stella formed a painting with vibrant colour in one of these groups. Even if she kept the picture for herself, the premise of Stella's friends seeing her art on Facebook holds a notion.

Regarding the photos of the paintings as an aesthetic bonus, for those that create art, think of the delight Stella received. The loves and likes on the post, I hope, added to her experience and brought her happiness. When we share our passions and likes and mean them, that's a way to contribute to others too. Positive comments can lift a heart, and add in the remarkable fact that the twenty people at the event held a shared experience of painting together.

The card game Magic:The Gathering is part of my life. That's another activity I feel happy to have. A friend named Ryan visited my home to help me proxy a legacy deck. Ryan gave me the benefit of learning how to print proxies so that other players can play Magic with cards they don't yet own or can't afford. The Magic community I know are pretty rad people, and Magic players know that people matter.

The kindness of a shared visit holds the value of inclusion both in the past, the present, and also the future. When we gather with people to interact, work, or play, we can enjoy people and appreciate their company. I have a prerogative to learn, love, live, thrive, create, play, and pray. Gathering with people extends parts of this prerogative.

Appreciating something and acknowledging the same thing is a key to gratitude. Something can be recognized, though gratefulness includes the appreciation of it. It results in a feeling, a positive feeling, and twists in and equation idea.

Awareness + Appreciation = Gratitude.

Gratitude = A Feeling of Gladness.

Where this book first started, I was a point of me being mad. I was ticked off and agitated by the fact that other people are angry that I'm glad. I'm aware that there are people who are potentially frustrated with me, and it seemed few wanted to help be part of our Freedom Solution. Our Freedom Solution is when we all can find financial, emotional, mental, spiritual, social, and physical freedom.

I know I neglect my health a lot by staying up late, though I want to make sure we can add and not detract from other people's wellbeing. The accumulation of time, knowledge, and experience are part of how we evolve, yet some things are like an instant. They change the entire game and sequence of events and can cause immediate ripples outwards. Some other stuff, though, can be like a glacial structure built and developed through gradual acquisition.

As we learn to encapsulate our fragmented moments of gladness as a memory, we also may think of the future technology that transfers our appreciation, and awareness directly into another person's mind. There is a notion that we can share a hug, a kind and real compliment or a gift of generosity at almost any moment of time. We can behave with kindness, goodness, and truth and infuse beautiful things, ideas, and energy into life if we choose to.

Some pre-formulated notions can also solidify fantastic parameters. Preparation for future events or people that we've not yet met are ideas to consider. As with our appreciations for others, as we adjust our actions and intents, we can slowly or quickly gather some perfect moments. We can secretly plan to surprise them with a seal of love and security, and one moment of time can be a choice for us to work for all.

How will you act and behave to work for the betterment of life? For what are you glad that you have that you want to share with others? What experiences or wisdom have you gleaned that you can recall and recount to another? How would you like to demonstrate appreciation to those that you admire or love? If you could have, do, or experience anything, what would those things be?

I hope you are glad and thankful for your life too. If you're reading this book, you have the luxuries of time, the ability to read (including sight, access to books, and a mind to process), and also the ability to appreciate another person's awareness. Good things can cause happiness and peace.

I think we'll do some things that we believed we could not.

Even if I've not met my gal, I don't have a car, and I still have so much time without communication, I also know that we're building our future. We shall thrive and communicate, and even if I haven't yet sold many books or can't even imagine providing for myself let alone a thousand people, I'm still glad I'm alive. I'm thankful we can dream and be grateful we are here on Earth.

Please remember that for which *you* are grateful. Please learn to be glad or thankful about anything or nothing. If you can learn to approach situations to be okay and thankful for any outcome, better results shall occur and be even that much more appreciated. Miracles will happen more frequently.

If we remember those who help us and those that need our help, have compassion and a willingness to provide for them, we can improve many lives and outlooks like ripples. Saying 'thank you' is a key phrase to remember to keep on the tip of your mind and tongue.

With that in mind, thank you. Thank you for allowing us to be, even if we never see. Thank you for reminding me to be like a drop of water in the sea. Thank you for allowing us to free the devotions held within the glee. And, thank you for reminding me too that the world of Earth includes seven billion others, including the allusions to Bri.

After forming this, I realize that there is one drastic error; I made a specialistic statement. There are far more than seven billion others; I had referred only to the human population. Forget not about the other animals, and dare not forget the spirits of those passed on, and those that are yet to come.

ROBERT KOYICH

HOLD THE BOND

If I am to hold true to this chapter's title, then I should clarify which bond I mean. Some connections are lingering covalently, yet electrons haven't exchanged.

There are people that I like and love, though I'm not so keen on being locked into full contact with some of them. If I'm not even clear if I could stay stable with another in a living confine, have I've been like a hydrogen atom who lost their two neutron pets?

When we spin different substances into water and create a solution, we may find ionization. I've treated myself very much like a free agent or single nodal point, yet I also wish not to be so noble. I'd like to be able to interact.

We can consider ourselves out there in the ocean of life, yet be right and sure that there are some salt and an expansive network of being out there beneath the surface. No matter how calm the water looks, substance, experience, resources, and activity are abundant.

On a tinier scale, the base protons and neutrons bind in the nucleus of an atom. I like the idea that there are a bunch of positive particles held together in the centre, yet also recall they are often with the neutral neutrons. According to physics and chemistry, there is no room for a negative particle in the core of an atom's nucleus.

Maybe we should heed the laws of nature in the metaphors of our lives and not annihilate. Reversely, it may be some view *us* as negative electrons that are not allowed into the core units of other people's atoms. We may be that negative cloud orbiting them. Think also of planets and their orbits around the stars. The moons around a world may blend of a multitude of distant suns, and how we spin around the central node of time in the centre of our galaxy.

There was an introduction to *The Simpsons* on episode 14 in season 15. It holds an animated sequence that spans outwards from within the inside of the family's home to a view from the outer atmosphere of Earth from space. The perspective extends extended outwards from Earth, past the solar system, and then, far beyond the Milky Way. Later, as the view becomes farther away, the multiple galaxies became the particles of atoms, then compounds and the building blocks of DNA. From the focus on a strand of DNA, the animation expands outwards to show a body's cells, and then the camera results as coming out of Homer Simpson's head. The picture then shows the family sitting on their couch from where the camera started.

Where are we as people on this planet if we are not in full relation, connection, and awareness of each other?

If we twist the words a bit more, relationships of family, a link of communication, and our consciousness hold our perceptual knowledge bases. We, as individuals in our bodies, know other people, animals, plants, or things can change us. If we become aware of anything, those objects change our thoughts purely by being part of consciousness. If we are in another's awareness, we have affected the context of their mind.

I hope you know that how you react when another tries to bond with you affects things; especially when we like them or want them to love us. These desires can cause complicating things to happen. If we draw in and attract those that dislike or feel negative about us, how will we choose to respond? How can we stop future adverse reactions if *we* are negative?

What happens when we instead become magnets for the fantastic thing that we enjoy? What happens when we attract miracles? How do we adjust our polarity to be that way?

There are people and things we like and prefer, though when we bond with them, some bonds will hold briefly. Other relationships may solidify forever. How can we secure a positive outcome? Sometimes what we like or enjoy may not be suitable or good for us.

We test and learn to know how we shall feel, think, respond, and we can do so by behaving with someone over a more extended period. Think of some people that you've liked on first meeting, and then later found yourself wanting to repel them and the very thought of their existence. What of those you've held dislike, and then later wish they never leave you and your life? It's a very particular concept and a very real, radical, and complicated thing.

If we are drawn in and attracted to another person and they don't want us to bond with them, there are times where we may have forced the connection. There are many cases we know where people have desired to bond and connected, yet we didn't want them to. I'm sure you've understood this; when we've liked a person a lot or felt drawn to them, some of them have then been 'meh' or even cynical about ourselves.

My mind goes to the intuition of fission and fusion and how they are metaphors. Fission (splitting) makes me think of how an unstable nuclear compound separates the atom and makes two entirely different substances. The reaction also produces a lot of heat and radiation that can be unhealthy for life. This nuclear reaction can be like a nasty divorce. It's mighty, affects many things, changes fundamental properties, and also may have started with the unstable material.

What I'd like to find is the *fusion* relationship.

When two lighter atomic nuclei form a solidified meld, a new compound arises. Fusion may cause the creation of excellent and powerful energy. I'd like to shape a full synthesis of the idea in the book *Beautiful, Do You Mind?*. If I form my lifelong mate through fusion, who shall it be?

Since this book is also the first in *The Fountains of Fortitude*, I think the title permits me to discuss how some beliefs I've held now affect me. For those that know part of my story, we know I'd gotten very focused and transfixed upon a famous singer who is almost entirely unknown to me.

Natalie Imbruglia was my obsession and focus for many years and very clearly the central fantasy I held for a significant portion of my adult life. When I was admitted to the psych ward the first time, I thought that she was birthing her and my twins and that was the reason I was at the hospital.

The first Fountain book, *Finding Natalie*, was initially intended to be shared with the world and lure Natalie to find me. I had soul stalked her, though, and still, it shows that decades after my first awareness of her I forced a bond with a person didn't want me. I put a lot of attention upon her and was trying to push the process to meet her. I don't even know if she knows who I am, yet I've had ideas she does. That's where my written journey started.

Today, I'm aware I have been inappropriate with my words, text, attitudes, and behaviours towards her, and that she must not be my objective. From the start of this chapter, I also know I cannot claim, wish, or intend to choose her as the one to bond with forever. I don't want to put a scoundrel like myself towards one that still holds my heart down and up from the vaults of my life. Natalie should not be sought out and used as a goal no matter what my truths are.

So if not to choose her, I also must remind myself of the other part; what will happen if another chooses me, and I don't want to bond with them? How will I react knowing that another person has thought such outrageous thoughts as I had for Natalie and that they're out there on Earth wishing and yearning to meet me?

For and from the other side, what famous people deal with, and how they cope with so much attention and focus on them is especially tricky when they are honestly only known through media? Within the Petri dish idea, a level of biology and not chemistry, what is happening when a bunch thoughts, nature, and exposure starts to seep outwards and develop a culture? Is what we're forming not a seed, yet instead, a mould?

Does a fuzzy coated layer expand outwards consuming things, or inversely, what if what I'm creating, thinking, and believing *is* the nourishment that should be protected and kept safe? Are the bacteria feeding on my life and removing the resources of my being?

Twisted in even further by the word 'culture,' I think about music and how Rap and Hip-Hop is a positive culture pervasive and robust. What if such a definite and beneficial culture view me as the enemy and wish to withhold and condemn my expansion? If I gave and got ejected from working as an emcee, perchance that's why I got moved to the authorship dish.

What happens with my strains of thought that are still alive and brought into the awareness of those who wished me removed? What about those who work to develop their practitionership and thrive within the game and my thoughts are fuel? Am I seed, or am I weed? I sometimes find myself at a crux where I know not how to proceed.

I feel fear about how juxtaposed time and ideas mix. There is a fear of how people interact like different chemical compounds as contact with some elements can create a new thing. Sodium in water is an explosive reaction. Some combinations can be dangerous. Some people connect and gel far more strongly or positively with others, and in full and constant contact assure an unbreakable bond.

For myself, I have spoken of wanting a girlfriend, yet the past fourteen years has had me living without a roommate or girlfriend other than when I had two cats. My cats were the two neutrons I referred to earlier and are a metaphor for how I was the one proton in my nuclear family. That sort of tells us I'm like Hydrogen.

I joke about religion now in that I could say that God is the Oxygen atom that splits itself, yet add the premise of Ozone as the Trinity. Trusting in God and Jesus as the living water in combination with us as individuals should not forget the Spirit and how the three of them together prevent those on Earth from being torched by UV rays.

Oxygen allows the two Hydrogen atoms to form water, yet, according to the Chemistry theory, the two Hydrogen atoms are bonded to and separated by the Oxygen atom. Rewinding to the fission idea, I think I've been attempting to fuse to establish Helium. Maybe water is a better objective? I honestly don't know.

Electrolysis is the process where electricity separates the chemical bonds of H_20 into Oxygen and Hydrogen gas. If we separate water back into Oxygen and Hydrogen, pairs of atoms return to their connective parts. I wonder if we find that elusive fission to make a nuclear family. Am I destined to fuse with others in a pair as a gas or water, or is it I combine with a female Hydrogen?

What shall the Fountains do though? They are links to water, yet when they separate, will the links connect people like I suppose they may? With one friend's feedback on *Seeds of Tomorrow*, she found the book optimistic, honest, and empowering. Forget how I want to bond; what about others and how you want to bond.

With couples, I'd like to find ways of strengthening some of those bonds. I never want to be the reason that separates a couple. With some relationships, there have been points I fear certain commitments could erode, and that is not something I want to do.

My parents each went through two divorces. It was their second marriage that resulted in me. Even though they both fundamentally changed their lives through divorce, I feel a released particle after their split. As an only child, I think of how I could have been an Oxygen, and they were my parental hydrogens as the first waters of my life.

We must start building life instead of just making ice cubes. I *don't* know who *my* lovestone is. Carbon gets to bond with all sorts of things, yet four out of three people can't do math!

Honestly, though, what if *I'm* Oxygen. Two bytes (16-bits) of information held within one shell of a body? I could interact with many different materials, though things could be affected. Maybe I should ship off from the chemistry and work on psychology? If we remind that salt also helps convey the messages through the neurons, I think we could send a different synaptic result. I don't want to bleach things and do like to keep things clean.

The two giraffes land face to face with a recoil of bass. *Sand to Silt* to tilt the foil from soil and geology of "how the eggs toil." We find a kind hen cooked up too high to make coffee to soften the potatoes with primo arigatos and how I do gift the sombre prose. What if the aardvark is transparent and concerned with the obtuse ones making advances to the dances of South America while skipping Central station towards Sham Shui Po? What if this winds the omission of teak to share the rhymes I speak?

I still don't know what bonds are solid ideas in mind. Perchance that's why I write; to cause new connections with the linear directions of text. I'd like to connect and bond with the future, and if it's okay to be with one specific lovestone, it could have been Uranium split. The three neutrons could've been our kids, and the separation would produce a lot of energy and radiation. Forever we would have been split.

Our kids could be the neutrons thrown from the reaction, and without control, other uranium atoms would split causing a chain reaction that could be deathly hazardous. This metaphor more accurately explained with real names is if Aeris was the neutron that I threw at Natalie, it could have split the idea into two separate particles and residue.

I've fantasized that if her and I married, she'd eventually want a divorce, and our three kids would be scattered with their energy and such to cause other separations. I don't want to split up like that. Is it best, perchance, that I stay as a single proton in my nucleus if I wish to have core family unity?

I'm still unhealthily over-obsessed and self-focused, though I'm also thankful I hone in on and dissect the lies, truths, and deceits. I may have put some of the worlds against me, yet as I make this secular repentance, I reveal what my faults and follies are. I must become aware of my mistakes before I can comprehend, accept, and process them.

Solemnly, I hope others find their books too. The incredible insights and attunement from the ability to write are so vital for those who want to know what life is all about. Through forming these books, I've come to a very long ways away from tossing ideas and thoughts off and onto the Internet. I've dug into feelings that have shredded my heart, yet they may have a positive consequence.

At this point, I must remind myself that there are forces of above and below that are other and part of a realm I've never experienced. I also must tell myself that many other people, compounds, and experiences have already bonded. Not all bonds are lasting, though. It's also true for some who have passed away that they will be attached to the psyche of another for always.

In regards to becoming aware of things, it's often easier to do when we are isolated. If we can separate ourselves from the others that are either forcing or attempting to bond with us, we can become clear about who and what we are. I know I am not an inert gas. There are substance and material to connect with, yet perhaps it's a conscious element to evade.

CHART A COURSE

Friends are valued and beneficial to my heart. I must remember that more often. Two had just dropped me off at home before I started writing this section; one is a male friend codenamed Jund, and the other is his girlfriend. I don't know her exceptionally well, though I know that the both of them are an amazing and rad couple.

The change from fantasy to fortitude cues forward to building a solid base. The title *Etched in Stone* also shows the shift in my inclinations from my past two or so years. I had not achieved very much success with the bookwork or sales up to 2018, though knowing that also sets my intent and actions. I regather my life and work and have faith in the higher powers of Earth and the cosmos.

An idea to rely on *The Sands of Yesterday* leads me to remind myself that I need a solid foundation like bedrock to build upon and not wishes, whims, and fancy. If I am to create foundational work, then I must secure it upon a rock-solid faith and system of universal life that is not just what I want.

Because going to church is not enough, sometimes, to say we know God or Jesus, I also wish not for martyrs or crucifixion. Christianity says Jesus died for us and that His doing so was the fatal sacrament that preserves our lives now.

My rested faith in our future also must be explicit before it ensues. There is power in making claims, commitments, and proclamations, though they must be backed up with action; one cannot claim to do things and then not act. Almost always, nothing will magically happen without effort.

The ideas of putting in the reps or honing one's craft are vital, though we also must couple those activities with other endeavours to strengthen their value. I have planned a lot and put out points of purpose and relationship, though I still have lacked some of the first crucial steps.

Regarding my books, I have written a bunch, though I've not yet formed pitches to sell the works. I may have made some progress through the maze, yet the first few dots need to be connected. Maybe the maze metaphor is not a good one?

Often mazes have an explicit entrance and exit, and if the metaphor holds, the entry could be the fixation I carried on about my dream girl. My wish is the end of the maze is the year 2053, and I'm in the room where I need to discover the secret places and pathways I need to find as we envision the middle of my maze.

The vision of the Glass House is one of those focused points of my future life, though I need to pass a great many pathways and corridors to reach there. If we build the Glass House, then I also must assure I get my books to market and sell them.

I hadn't, when written, yet known what value or purpose the content of my Fountains books have for readers, yet I know that selling books is a multi-win. I've yet to understand why anyone would want to support those wins, and although I'm not clear of the wisdom of the idea, the question is: "What would happen if I made myself famous for generating sales?"

I had achieved notoriety in Vancouver when I was trying to be a rapper/MC, and that path almost led to my death. I know some of the reasons linked to my drug use, how I showed a blatant lack of morals, and how I was projecting myself as being far more significant than I was, and though I also was deplorably out of bounds with my thoughts, actions, and attitudes I admit I abused and breached many boundaries.

There were some people, though, who understood my lack of control and mental issues and knew I do have some positive merits. There's a reminder that quite a few people do and did love and honour me, and I know this because I'm still alive. I had, though, polarized the community in both definitions of the word.

With my current bookwork, I have the idea that my books will only have value to others if they read them. How do I get people to understand and process them? At this point, I've found that a very few have read the books and that those people are people that like, care, or want to support me.

There is value in the books, yet I don't know yet how to articulate that to another that has no idea who I am. With the fame idea, I also incept the concept because I know there is additional value in the books if people know or have interest in who I am.

Is this a double-sided piece of the puzzle? That if people read the books because they know me, they will understand more, and that people who want to know who I am will learn? I paralleled this with movies in a conversation.

Some people will watch anything and everything from a director because of who the director is. Some other people will watch a film because of what the movie is regardless of who is the director because it's a good movie. My idea is to create books people will want to read because they are both intriguing books and also because people will gain by reading them.

I do not so much want fame, yet instead, am plotting and planning what we can do if attaining popularity would facilitate the channel of book sales. If I can continue to create and live, maintain my principles and commitments, and grant grace and prosperity, then how I can convey these ideas to others as something people want to support?

It's almost like I *have* to push for being very well known to allow the Seed Fund, the Glass House, and my self-sustained income to be things that manifest. My lack mentality, at this point, narrows my view down to how can I achieve those goals? The answer is, form a plan and start taking the steps.

Diana (a past Toastmaster) brought me an idea that the first step is to devise or develop a pitch for my books. This chapter is processing that and from where I stemmed the title *Chart a Course*. My first instinct is to describe what the books are, though they're all about my thoughts and me. Who's interested in that!? (Hint: not so many people).

With the Providing Point ideas, I've vied for people to support because of what we can do with the books. That's part of the book's allocated purpose, though why would that be valuable to another? If people want to pledge to a charity, is it not more efficient to give money to the charity and not buy a book?

Do my books land in the self-help section? Do they tell people how to run a productive business? They indeed don't demonstrate how to improve one's health, how to fix issues in a romantic relationship, or even how to invest one's money. The Fountains books don't even explicitly teach others a valuable skill such as how to write, how to market services, ideas, or products, or even clearly show people how they can find their dreams to come to fruition. I seem not to understand or relay explicitly valuable skills or formulas for others to follow or use.

What my books do convey, though, is a series of thoughts that insight one to think deeper about some social issues and other concepts. My books hopefully shall instill a bit of compassion and kindness, and by discussing some of the frustrations and fears I share, a few delicately placed ideas or points of knowledge can incite hope or understanding for another.

I seem to think we can glean a great deal by forming these books, though how can I encourage or invite people blankly to my books to learn what they hold? I had become so well known in the past through the channel of music and being ejected from the rap game, that I think I may be tainted goods. My reputation from the past still holds fragments and shards seemingly aimed at my heart.

I know I didn't succeed in the Rap game and that I'm not

suited to live in that ecosystem. I'm not an extraordinary socialite with levels of confidence and skill required for surviving there. The hate and animosity aimed at me caused some of my fear and insecurities, and I also do not often feel brave or bold.

If I hold away from the world because of my cowardice, how will I comply with the will of many and stand up for many more than myself? If I am inclined to think I will stand up for some, yet how does sharing books with people support that belief? It's a more suitable channel for conveying my thoughts compared to music.

The path of authorship is far different than the music game and suits my more introverted personality. I set my wants aside sometimes, and still twist and turn guidance into the fuel for our future. My fear of condemnation has had me wishing to break free of almost everything, isolate crucial points of fact, and find a way of empowering much more than myself in a positive, peaceful, and prosperous way.

I hold value in fairness and a belief that if I am to earn readership, I may need to risk becoming very well-known again. How will I learn, act, and behave to ensure we generate positive results?

What I write may be openly scrutinized as to what my thoughts have been, yet I come from a past where written words hold far more permanence. I've grown much since living in Vancouver, and even if I have carried corrupted thoughts, my ethical stances secure.

There is a line in a recording made back then by friends that said: "Make it through to the knowledge side / Natalie, kids, and a dope-ass ride." I know that music is prophetic, yet did that 2001 reference mean that I'd shift from making music to what I'm doing now? The line secretly calls my delusions back with a blend to remind us I still don't know.

What if *The Sands of Yesterday* is put into the crucible and melted into a new form? Would it be glass, or can we dare return the sediment into stone again? What if we allow all the *Fragments of Intent* to cement the heart back into where it formed? It would not be the same piece of work, yet what of Kintsukoroi? Can we fabricate something even more beautiful from the fractured remains?

How can something be etched in stone if there is no stone upon which to carve the words? Is text the time muddles in a metamorphic heart? Are these shorelines of writing a process something of which to weave, deceive, or leave? If we are brought forth as being eternal, who else will ever believe?

Is it true that it's a stone upon which my thoughts etch upon instead of a rock? Why is God the rock? I should build on a reliable foundation, yet I'm still not clear if my fountains have eroded parts of the truth away.

I seem to think I've bathed my being in the waters of the world while neglecting to remind myself my work is still like a glacier on a mountain. Mountains *are* rock and stone. Dare it to be that I'm skiing on the glacier separated from the foundation? Has my work kept me away from knowing God even though it's stability for which I yearn? Maybe I should stop skiing and dig deep into the Earth.

If Earth is where God's humans are, is it that we're helping this planet with my past, present, and future? What if God doesn't want me on this planet? Christians would say that 'let God's will be done' and that we should accept that. How can one condone another for wishing life to be entirely removed? If God created me, then why would he design me to insight so many mistakes, errors, and contempt? Have I been set up for defeat, or is there a secret plan?

If we are to chart a course, then I must know where we want to go. That's where my future wishes and wants are my guideposts, and I still hope to find kind people that can welcome my ideas. My challenge is to know where I want to be, and then the question is how to get there.

Who *are* the ones that will help us sort out a collective Freedom Solution? Initially, I wanted to use the Seed Fund as a promotional idea to generate sales as a win/win idea. It held that held people would be more likely to buy my books if they knew it funded a charitable cause.

If people want to help a charity, though, they can give directly with more efficiency. The manipulation tactic of having people buy my books to have the Seed Fund thrive was partially self-interested. Andrew was right; it seems pretty scummy.

If I shift my reason for pushing sales for my gain, is that a more socially acceptable strategy though? If I gain a monetary benefit from sales, then there is additional motivation for me to push for sales. I still think we can do far better things with these books.

In chapter eight of *A Distant Glimmer*, I made an income declaration. I made a hedge because if I committed 100% to Seed of all book earnings, I would be working for 0% personal earnings from my work. The final choice was heeding Gary Vaynerchuk's advice and putting 51% of the profits to the cause. To sell something, though, they need to be valued.

How can I tell people that the books are valuable beyond what they generate financially? That's where I wish not to be deceptive. The ability to sell is vital, though according to my ethical wants, I'm intending on earning my audience through trusted recommendation. I prefer that my reputation may generate interest or acceptance and that my works speak for themselves. It's a glacially slow process, though if my books are so much about my ideas, and not marketable knowledge or advice, I will require such a means to acceptance.

The results up to now have not been much, yet my foolishly optimistic self still grasps at hope and fate. I believe they hold purpose, though I need to figure out why people should read and buy the books and tell them why. If my compass guides correctly, and we draw the map correctly, why would anyone go searching for treasure if there is none?

The focus should be giving, not trying to sell the map to people or trading for the compass. It's your map of life, and your guides are the compasses. I should be making sure if you bought the map and compass to help guide you in how to use them, you also can enjoy the search as something worthwhile.

SIAMO INTERNAZIONALE

I love Earth, I appreciate other cultures, and I love languages. Life carries our truths forward, and as I write, I find that there is strength in shared beliefs. My values of inclusion and multiculturalism infuse different languages, though I've sometimes used them to obfuscate.

From a deeper understanding and appreciation of my core self, I may sound vain or obscene. I like the people at Snowpeaks, the Thursday night Toastmasters group, for how they remind me how Earth does hold many different people. It's radical how we can help and teach people more about English and interaction, yet I must learn too.

My work includes many more than a few, though I'm the one who presses the keys. Each edit layers, and as I use the banner Introversial for my work and though, the Fountains books seem to be the primary product. At this point, I'm the only person working for Introversial, yet the claim is the Fountains are public.

With awareness and connotation held, some may admire a fountain, there can be statues to adorn them, yet not all should drink from them. On travel, I've seen fountains in many public squares for the benefit of all in the town. In 2017 and early 2018, Snowpeaks meetings brought me a vital and keen place like a public square where I prepared a speech titled *The Seed*.

When I was a member of Snowpeaks, Japanese, German, French, Portuguese, and Dutch were represented, with three Spanish speakers also part of the group, tough from three different countries. The Thursday night group members all interact and speak English, yet I was the only one of two whose first language is English.

Language and culture are one way to remind us that we are not alone or the same with our comprehensions. Think also of locational differences between people. We can start at home locally or provincially, to nationally, and then even intercontinental. As the human population is now, we are bound to Earth, yet that might not always be the case.

My Dad and step-mum live in Australia, and when I was in grades five through seven, my Mom, Dad, and I lived in Hong Kong. I don't know Cantonese beyond an exceptionally few simple words, though I loved living in Hong Kong and it was a wondrous experience. I'd like to visit there again. I also lived in Australia, and that links to how I'm thankful to know I am allowed to be in that country too.

I am a person who is appreciative of different cultures, though drugs corrupted me. My thoughts and insecurities put barriers between myself and some others, and I'm still learning my mind. Revealing parts of my psyche that mayhap should be hidden, I've had a scary issue with racism.

I don't like racism, especially the slurs, the hate, and the violence stemmed from it. I have been aware of and exposed to some racial issues, and those experiences had tainted my thoughts. My theories about telepathy include premises that not all of the ideas in my mind are my own, though some would contest that. I also don't want to blame my mental corruption on drugs, though know that they have played a substantial role.

The doubters and believers mingle in the Contialis. If I'm to argue with the doubters and spin in my self-analysis and self-awareness, my thoughts twist back to how love is the solution. I believe that by learning more of my absolute truths and, as I recommend to you, writing them down, might help clear up some confusion.

I wrote in the book *Built from Within* yesterday night after a stressful evening. What I wrote was sourced from my insecure and doubtful side. I mentioned how we can control our language in different ways, and how it's easier to write our intended meaning than it is to speak sometimes. It's also easier to manage our spoken words than our thoughts, yet our truths may spill out through Freudian slips. The subvert twist, though, is that it's our thoughts that can have the most potent effect on our lives even if we don't speak them.

We live with our thoughts every day. I hold my written work as a way to share myself, yet my written words are more secretive than my thoughts ironically. Few know my written truths, yet many have assumed things about me from what they've heard. With my firm belief in telepathy, I wonder how much of Ashley's opinion is right.

Ashley believes that our body language carries a stronger weight than what we say and that no one else can hear anyone else's thoughts. I've often thought myself to be a psychic beacon and additionally believe that thoughts and feelings are manipulated easily with sensitive thinkers. There are knee-jerk reactions we may feel about things and physical, emotional, and mental reflexes are a definite thing. Maybe it's what people see of us when they are approaching and not our thoughts?

As I live on my own alone in my apartment writing these books, I am that, alone. Living in the thought realm and having no one to talk to, it's difficult to escape from my thoughts when I get diverted onto a negative thought train. I have no ground wire to dissipate the negative static electricity of my mind sometimes, and the friction of life can cause a buildup of energy. The impulsive releases of energy are sparks that can shock a mind.

We must be aware that Earth needs to be a well-oiled machine. Communication and positive reciprocation lubricate our beings into slithering goodness outwards from ourselves. I believe that things can change our attitudes, and though it's electrical, the idea of magnetism holds a different polarity. It's best to recall that gravity and nuclear bonds exist too.

All these electrons are coursing through the water of life, and if electricity, a flow of negatively charged energy, can separate water into the separate Oxygen and Hydrogen, we also must be careful. We could cause an explosion by igniting the Hydrogen when it's in its gaseous state.

Gravity holds liquids in their containers, yet the seriousness of the issue is that I think I often miss my cue. Are we digging deeper into the layers of our life by allowing me to nudge the cursor right along the page continually? Are the Fountains shifting and changing directions of the loom that she weaves; asking Jordan too what the Red Sea could find within the freshly fallen leaves?

Water is life; that's a universal Earth thing. We don't know if other planets need water to live, yet it's an assumption. This planet holds water as one of the most vital components of life as we know it, yet that's where I shift back to humans and the structures we've made.

We've built a world where ideas and the information have accumulated. Some ideas recycle, and some are stored away in our histories unknown. Some other parts of life held within the realms of vague ideas and awareness have zero mass. The notions of time and space carry no physical weight, while the purpose of the spirits and souls that have also died theoretically also hold substantial importance with their current activity. Technically, an idea or thought hold no physical form either, yet we know these things can change matter.

Systems of culture and religion are omnipresent. Ingrained also are the notions of chemistry, biology, and physics into many culture's ideas. The ideas of business are also inherently linked to human dynamics and interaction, even if there isn't a physical monetary system. Humans are the dominant species regarding technology and stored or recorded information. We also know that. The idea of life, though, doesn't need to track money, science, or belief. There can be the argument that life (in the full animal kingdom) is instinct, thought, and action. Intuition is a premise and ability that has eternally linked some.

I'm pretty daft actually. Because I'm a human and have a

computer to type on, I have been abusing the ability to infuse my ideas and theories into the minds of another. If our thoughts build from instinct, our words and language layer upon our beliefs, and our desires guide how we attempt to manipulate life, then I remind myself to trust myself and use my words for good. The idea to work for good is a biased idea also.

Where does the source of everything come from that would assure that anyone would be aware of anything I think, say, or write? The astronomers say there are millions of galaxies and billions of years of time outside of ourselves. Others have said there are infinite Universes that exist outside of our mixed reality. I am one person, we also all exist. If you perceive this in any way, even if not yet in a printed form, or even as one to read this book, you are alive. That also could be a lie. Perchance you have not yet been born, or you are a spirit of one long dead that attunes to the magic.

Where my language blends in is partly sourced from an international game. It is an Earth idea, and it's also presumably not known by many people on Earth. The codes I use include on colour referencing; a compelling notion of perception, yet math is also a prevalent idea on Earth. I combine lines and hope their principles may be understood in other worlds, even if not consciously in the non-living spirit world.

The downside about language is that only those who understand or know the words they read, hear, feel, or speak will comprehend them accurately. It may be my responsibility to learn, yet I also intuit, even to my chagrin, that it is also my responsibility to teach.

My ethics will change, and the changes in my values shall also affect how I communicate. Sometimes we may be alone, though I put my trust in a faith that we shall evolve. We are responsible for our own choices; there are numerous influences that direct our decisions. It's a choice to elaborate on our lives.

By setting objectives, I may not achieve them, yet I make the goals anyhow. They give me a point to direct towards, and

I accept some ways of life may never be known. There also is the case that I won't do some things and that once something has happened, it's happened.

Do we get to choose what we do, or are we each having to follow our linear responses of time reacting to our perceptions; our views that sequentially guide us forward to the explicitly non-avoidable points? Or, do some things entirely unchangeable allow us to hone out from pre-conceived ideas outward to never present moments of time that hold in the awareness of a single climb? It may have stopped before we never encountered the rhyme.

Will we have already passed that moment that just happened and never be allowed to experience it again? What happened when time travel took us back to before now to live the moment again? Déjà True?

Or, are we floating along in our shells of bodily awareness gradually understanding that they set ideas from the galaxy in a teardrop? Is emotion only an animal thing? Do non-living things not hold psychic energy by being the awareness of another living creature? Do we as humans unearth truth?

Am I able to start this sentence with any other word as the second word in English and still have it be grammatically correct? Do you dare me to be eternal? Who can assure it to be true? Certainly not myself. I am a human who is often baffled by the idea that I am.

It's an intentional lure to make us think. I don't try to invoke thought. I know, though, that I do. Who is the first name that you remember? Who is the most recent person that you thought of afterwards? Is it the same person? *"We can't talk about that"*-Cam, of Division G.

What of the Round Table? Is Arthurian legend known across cultures? If we only understand or comprehend English, how will we communicate with those that don't? There are some words in English that everyone knows that I never want to hear or think. Some words are spoken too often that no one has ever imagined, yet some people have never felt anything other than that.

What if we live as if our entire being is already known? What if what we don't know about ourselves is right and we never come to understand until we meet another who reveals every one of our truths? What if what we think is untrue is fortified fact? That's where our communications can assist.

I recall my auntie Bonnie saying: "What if we all think you're an ass, Rob?" I know I've indeed been treated like one. What if you are pure, amazing, awesome, and real, and no one will believe you? What happens with the involution of all things of an unknown being is brought into our awareness when we have no one to tell? What truths can I convey? What it you never know I have or will exist?

I still don't know.

Shape our world. Hold your love. Share. Create! Learn? Yes. We must. Know too that we may never know, yet that you know, and also that you may always remember.

"Of all that I have remembered, I haven't forgotten a thing."

---*Cliff*
Roulston

It's straightforward to focus in and be aware of nothing but oneself and one's thoughts. We're not solo, though. We are each a central node of a conscious being that is part of multiple cosmic realms. Though this chapter's title says 'we are international' we are not just that. We each are part of everything. All things, thoughts, entities, matter, and time are part of a whole. It is wise for us to remember others and the fact that we're all integrated.

We share a universe, it is diverse, and it is not just for us alone to know. Get out there into the world of Earth and sip in some of the fresh waters. There may be some things yet for us to learn and share, yet there is an exciting twist of our planet; perchance some other species would like to visit here and have not yet been to Earth before.

I'M IMPATIENT

From the review of *Finding Natalie* by Miss Allin, there was advice to form the books as I had started them; like a journal. In line with that guidance, it was December 10th, 2017.

I'm impatient with this work and process! Up to December 2017, only $42.70 generated from online sales. I am eager, yet there's a layer of repentance also; I've not done enough. My small actions have pushed some away, and I've used some people. With friends, they should not just be customers, yet of customers too, there must be more value for them. My goals seem to have teleported me and my work to where we now are. What have I done?

I'm impatient about the results of my work and also have an edgy feeling of not knowing where to put the plow. I can write, though that isn't enough. There needs to be a definite purpose and intent to form results of, even so, Full Seed.

My impatience finds me to need help from others to achieve Full Seed and note there is a time-sensitivity too. Each day that books aren't selling, each additional day that money is not provided for others in need. Even though the Providing Point Patreon earnings go to others, if there aren't earnings, then what may we give?

I'm so impatient with my school work and process! I had an exam the next day and was on the computer because I was too agitated about my situation not to form this. I want to market, earn, share, and seed future yields, yet I'm also not clear where to ask for sales?

As the Fountains are my processing journals, thank you for letting me sort this out. I've written some of the plots and plans in notebooks, though the advice is to share the schemes, ideas, wishes, and dreams with others and write this here.

School is beneficial, though finding out how we can achieve Full Seed has a time pressure and stronger importance than overpreparing for an exam.

The situation compels me.

The books must have value for readers beyond just the function of what their earnings do. [Habit 4: Think Win/Win] compounds. If we sell 500,000 books that would provide for some, yet what gain will those 500,000 readers receive? If you write, think of what you'd love to share with that many people.

What lessons or ideas can we share that will improve many lives and not just our own? The premise to give is vital, and it's an ethic that many hold. What I need is my value to be to provide and earn the right to be read. My work must have value beyond a functional purpose to supply people with resources.

Some people don't want to force others to learn or what to do while some people thirst for knowledge or ideas they've never heard of or read before. Still, some others may yearn for a story to read and escape from their lives. What my wants and wishes are are not enough to be used as a channel to persuade people to help a cause, even if not their own.

The desire to give others ethical principles may be amplified, yet that requires kinship with those ideas and prerogatives that are seeds of their own. As much as I can't just wish for others to align, I can nudge some line back onto pathways for positive forward motion.

The invitation to read a book is another challenge. With books, it's not just a monetary investment or a give; the time to process is another thing. It must be a win/win. If you've given me your time to read what I've formed, there best be a gain for yourself too. If the books are so much about me, then how or why will that have value to another who doesn't care or have interest in who I am or what I think?

My attempts at being poetic or insightful are not a successful lure. The actual derived value of myself may even be not what I write, yet instead who I am and what I can do for the world regardless of my books.

A desire to earn a profitable life is overtly money focused and my passion for my works and words to have an impact seem like a fruitless effort. An urge to create and figure out life, even if my so exceptionally self-focused and seemingly delusional one, is a driving motive.

The Freedom Solution of doing what we want to do veritably has been the impulse of these books. Even if my promises are for others, the primal urge and source of these books is impatience and dissatisfaction with how life is for others and myself.

Finding Natalie was my dissatisfaction with decades of unresolved feelings, *Searching for Tomorrow* was from malaise with not knowing my path of life, and *From the Valley to the Fountain* was from my impatience with reaching the goals of the first two books.

I fueled *Seeds of Tomorrow* with the displeasure of disparity and me wishing for results, *Fields of Formation* stemmed from being unhappy with how life was mid-2017, and *A Distant Glimmer* was me pissed off that I've not done more.

Now, in *Etched in Stone*, I'm still agitated that I've not accomplished more with what my wishes and wants from the first six books are. Though we remember this, we find ourselves in the present and remember we may make a new start.

Many ways of forgotten days pass into the present. I know some people still need a home, and if we can't use my ideas to find homes for some of those people, then why do I do this? My personal needs are few, and *I* don't need to worry about what I want. I have my coffee, my ciggies, my home and I have my friends, my family, my work.

What I also need, though, is to remember is that I can help our communities in ways other than shelter, resources, and text. If I can share some good ideas and conversations about how to build and help create and develop understanding and compassion, then those may be values worthy to convey.

Ask yourself some of these questions please? How do you like helping people? Do you prefer to help people with their social or emotional needs, or with resources? Do you want to support one or a few people, or help many? What do you have an abundance of that you'd like or love to share? What can you give today, or in the future? Would you prefer to give your time, your knowledge, your attention or your direct personal support?

Do you want to be recognized for your contributions, or are there ways you can secretly help? Are there other people who need or want your help? Though some may not like it, I do add; in what way, if any, would you like to be compensated for your help? Do *you* need help? With what do you need help? Have you asked for help?

These are three different questions that don't always come from the opposite side of the fence. Some people may seem not to need help from anyone, though genuinely require it. Then too, I remind myself, some people may look like they need help and not want any from anyone. I mustn't assume another would accept support if offered.

The question of "Do you need help?" can open pathways to doors for guidance to arrive. I think we may need to ask ourselves those three question again. Do we need help? With what do we need help? Have we asked for help?

What if someone does need help and has explicitly asked? Both sides can view this question; the one who needs support, and the one who's asked for assistance. Sometimes people ask us for our help, though how do we respond? Do we look for excuses, or are we thankful to have the ability to help?

What of those times when we've not asked for help, and someone tries to help us? It's not always appreciated. I mustn't be so arrogant or assumptive that another needs my support or advice, and I also mustn't be a fool to think that I can't do more to give to other people.

My impatience lies in that muddle. I'm not clear on how I can help those in need if I don't put in a substantial effort to put my work out to the world to allow others what they need. For some friends, a conversation is what they need. For some other friends, maybe the way I can help them is to give them some space and leave them alone.

If we can't or don't want to help with resources, we can find other ways to support. We can engage with others and help them with their dreams, and we can use our care and knowledge to encourage them with their work and projects.

We *can* bring ideas and connections together to network for a combined future. We also can bridge the space of time between our checkpoints and lives by sharing our hearts. Even though I'm isolated and separate from so many things and people, I refuse to give up. My bullish and persistent mind and soul refuses to stop and not forge new pathways and points of thought.

My written work *hasn't* yet gained a vast readership, though I intuit I must surrender to the process while still planting future yields. Though I can feel sad that I've not earned so much for others, I continue to progress and persevere. Honestly, I wonder how much my passion, obsession, or obligation is doing within this work. I often call myself neurotic and write off the ideas to move forward.

What are your creative endeavours? Do you write or record things? Do you draw, sing, or play an instrument? Are you a person who deems themselves non-creative? Do you cook meals or organize events? Are you a public speaker or coach? I'd be quite surprised if you're a business person as you'd probably be focused on your business and not reading my books!

For an inverted part, are you a person who thinks collectively and are hearing the channels of thought from the person who is reading this book? My bizarre notion even knows that some of you are not yet a person who is again on the same plane of existence. There are other forces at work on Earth that is not from our galaxy.

Am I too allusive to the realms of thought not yet formed? You may have read this whole book at some point in the future, yet maybe not as it developed. I also want to assure that what you've learned from it didn't even exist in the printed form until months after this moment.

Maybe you've read the entire saga up to and past the next book *Open to Fate*? That may not have been able to be true yet, though we also don't know what the future holds. I hope you have some wishes that have yet to unfold in 2019 and beyond as well.

I'm impatient, yet optimistically persistent. I know I can't forecast what happens with these books, though I keep them evolving and refine them. The *Sands of Yesterday* was being revised again and was released June 4th, 2018. At that point, *Fragments of Intent* needed to go through a rewrite, yet in 2018, for myself, I'm okay.

Though others may not understand I know this process is going too slowly, we've yet to earn money for others and myself. The Purpose of Providing Point is to provide, and it calls my heart the fact I've not housed others yet.

What would happen if I gave up entirely on working on these books? What would happen if I relied solely on the Universe to do that that it will? What if I yield entirely to doing what I intuitively deem best for only myself? I don't want to take that path. I need to keep making forward motion for life.

Will the Universe and world of Earth make good use of my creative instinct and have the correct connections linked by fate and destiny? What if I only typed what my soul yearns for until the point of 2025 when we reach the inner walls? What if the devotion I've made is actually in the suit of hearts and not the spade that I believed it to be?

What of the crows who assure peace holds? What of the dove that seemed to neglect my forgotten love? With a full breath, I hold the gull to pull the Kookaburra Max into the flax and keep the tracks in the racks of the packs. I'm impatient about her too as I haven't yet been able to fly far away from that moment of above. It was like her spirit was floating down from a dimension of pure heaven down to my own earthly body.

There can be Heaven on Earth, yet today I heard that angels are not divine, that they are merely God's servants. I thank God for allowing me to know there is a subtle union that tethers me to tomorrow, yet the rhymes would say the three feathers may not be from the same species. I give them to her anyway.

How can I claim these Fountains to be of Fortitude? They still seem like Fantasy. Should it be Yesterday, then Faith, then Fortitude, and then Fantasy? Do I need to be secure to reach my fantasies as a real thing? I may rely upon the yesterdays that build faith, and that in fortified endurance, I can move forward and into our future.

We allow now to be then again when the signs of life seem to guide us into what I should say to assure I meet my wife; no matter who she is. The pull between creative integrity and artistic freedom find the waters reveal some concealed snow and ice. It may cause some people to slip and slide, yet I also best not perform doughnuts in the parking lot.

Of the planets, Venus is said to be the bringer of Peace while Mercury is who's closest to the sun. I was to call her Aeris as my Mother would be Earth, and the Father is sometimes called Mars. It's a twist with my family that my mother is an Aries; I only just noticed Aeris, my daughter's name, is an anagram of that.

I doubt myself and my future and wonder if I'm just an extra. When we see movies, countless people don't have a speaking role, yet the movie crossover also reminds you that I don't necessarily want to be a star. I don't want to have to act, yet if I do compete for 39 days, I'll need to develop my ability to see through the lies. That may still be a cube of ice to chew.

The most primary people in my life? What does it matter to you? You maybe don't even know I exist. You may be one who's believed in me before I believed in myself. My parents are primary people for me; that includes my step-parents. I don't like playing favourites! My cousins are cool links, yet I'm distant. Uncles and Aunts hold a part in my heart, and it seems I put my friends after my family.

It's weird that most of the people I can meet up with and interact aren't family. I have no family in town yet refuse to quit. I'd also like to include those that I've not met in real life who've influenced me with their music, books, online work, or guidance.

I've been seeded by many I've not yet met that hold amazing and monumental influence on Earth. I don't even compare. Though, I've thought to have the audacity to write what I have! How could I believe that I'd ever meet a famous star and provide for thousands other than myself when I've not even been able to yet provide for myself?

Another miracle, though. I have already written what I have! I've been alive long enough to record 250+ tracks and put books online. I've been able to live long enough to be here to type this.

What if they erased everything I've formed? What if we achieve my audacious claims and proclamations? What if my fears, insecurities, and paranoias are needed to have planted fields in the Universe? How do we allow my plow to be pulled ahead by myself living myself twenty years further from now?

The consect still has a grasp on me and what I do. I cannot express this enough to you. It's not funny what one told me, and though it moulds me well outside the tides of thought, some others allow us the fact that both Heaven and Hell vie for the pacts we use to counter the spell. How shall we dredge up the secrets that you need to know without tipping the balance?

A SHARD OF MISDIRECTION

As solidified as a direct counsel and guide, it's true the facts are pacts made by us to reside in the tide. She knows she doesn't know who I am, and the gemstones cannot accurately express enough how the puffs pass onto the next.

These involutions share the distributions of time's sands as we try to control me. I also fear I'm not speaking the truth and cannot prove the equation. There is still far too much uncertainty, and I wish not for their coercion.

What if I am telling the truth and love, just not in the way that we shall believe? Being told things so often and with such contradictory statements and viewpoints of what love is may confuse.

My ideas of the plots and plans are pinned up on the wall against me. I may have broken a heart, yet still, I must not impart that well enough. I dare not subscribe to cos signing for them as the energy is too apparent. It feels like lost love and trust, yet the respect levels shown are in entirely different ways. I don't sense them all.

As for me? I feel uncertain, edgy, and honestly profoundly concerned and excited for my wellbeing. The overload and overwhelm I sense sometimes tell me that they should NOT be trusted. That applies not only to one person, yet rather others too as I am not always a good judge of character.

This chapter is from a different point of view and direction than where the Fountains series started. Additional clarity has formed regarding my work, yet what and why I do what I do shift. The context of four different points mixed paramount significance to myself, and my life resounded.

Four major life events, attitudes, and energies in vastly different quadrants of people occurred the day I wrote this chapter. I shall keep other people's secrets safe and not reveal personal information, yet the facts are blatantly not known to have yet shown.

Jessy visited. She is fantastic and seems radically calm, bright, and fresh. Jessy is the love quotient regarding the romantic and potential girlfriend part of late 2017 and the first half of 2018. She is kind, cheery, and attractive and makes my heart feels light, happy, nervous, and glad when we meet.

My intents with Jessy are to engage in communication and interactions with her because of how I like how I feel; happy, light, and squeamishly good. Jessy is 'like' love, and I don't know her very well. I am, though, highly intrigued and alluded to meet up with her. She is a super positive person that I'm thankful to connect with again.

The second love part of the day I wrote this is more Kantian and far more profoundly rooted. The person that I wrote to in the chapter *Community and Consect* in the book *Fields of Formation* seems like a dearly tainted love connection. She has a drastic effect on me, my attitude, and my energy.

I have been chat trapped by her, and I don't trust her. It's partly from the things she says of other members of our family. I feel enslaved when bonded to her, and I don't like how invasive they had been. The way they are a love connection is that I sacrificed a severe amount of my freedom, attention, sanity, and safety to choosing to connect.

My time and heart, to them, may not be understood, yet what I don't like is how it seems they are forcing me to love them when I don't feel happy or glad to hear from them. Obligation and forced love is NOT a kind thing, and I like and enjoy kind and peaceful attitudes and people.

The third person is a kind and social link to a different rational and real connection. The friend has helped me out with my creative endeavours with respect, communication, and resource links. When we meet up and converse, they have been very generous to me, and I think they are a safe person.

This third person graciously shares themselves because they are glad that God has given them what they have. They deem it a kind and proper thing to share and use to help others with what they've been blessed. They've helped with car rides and friendship because they want to. Sometimes I have a concern people support because they think they are obliged to do so and not that they want to.

The fourth section stems from one of the Magic shops. The emotional and soulful stress from earlier in the day was evident in my chest at the shop. I had an extreme nervousness and instability in my heart from the family member I mentioned.

Contact with Magic friends can bring happiness, gladness, and thankfulness to my heart. The chance to break away from the stress from earlier in the day was appreciated. There also are car rides home from safe friends that I much enjoy.

Quite a few people have helped drive me and the fact of not needing to worry if safe or not walking, *and* having the chance to speak my heart matters a lot to me. I want to be around more people that I feel safe and free to talk to with and about.

My understanding of obsession is a unique viewpoint. I have obsessed about some people in my life, and I realize how inappropriate that is. If karma and reciprocation is a definite thing, then I see how wrong I was to be so obsessed about Natalie. Perhaps unconditional love has conditions.

Linked through unity, love and respect also includes kindness and giving people the space to live their lives on their own. I don't like some of the obsessive focus, attention, and attachment that people have had for me. When a person tells you that they want to stop a conversation, it is kind and respectful to thank them and allow them to carry on with their days, and sometimes, lives.

Love is not trapping someone and making them do what

you want them to do. Love is allowing someone the space to be who they are, to let them speak to you what they like and love, and to enable them to feel happy and thankful to know that you want to talk with them.

If you love someone accurately, they will want to be around you, to connect with you, and to reach out to you with happiness, gladness, and not due to obligation. I'm sorry for not being able to love some in the way they want me to, and I also don't want to like you because I need to.

I want to like and appreciate people in action, and with the amount of pressure put on me, I need to keep some out of contact to allow myself to live my life and process. She is loved, though I can barely interact or speak sometimes.

I keep myself out of contact and don't want some people in my life on a daily basis. I like distant love, not the active shackles that it seems to be once in a while. Natalie would be clear about that too. Why would she ever want to allow me the chance to hear her honest voice and let me into her life with the level of obsession I've had with her.

I think Natalie knows that I'm not healthy for her, and she also knows that she needs her freedom and space to be. I put far too much attention and focus upon her, and it's clear to me that if she does know who I am that she also would know about my obsession. Obsession and infatuation is not a healthy form of love.

Maybe my cousin's fierceness and ferocity are from the point of real true love? It had been a tremendous and formidable force that seemed to squish out every possible chance for my life to be my own. It feels like she wanted to control and trap me and not let me live free and happy. I didn't feel loved; I felt ensnared.

I felt forced and contained, and even I hold a deep love and respect not shown conclusively. I accept and believe respect and love to be, yet if there are five different love languages, we are positively speaking differently. I can say "I love you," and mean it, though I accept or understand I need to show it, not just claim it.

I cannot assert genuinely, and in a way you understand, that I want to be happy, that when I force saying 'I love you,' it doesn't seem real. Instead of others understanding I have and show love with my actions and not words, even writing seems not to convey the truth.

Different types and feelings of love need to be learned. Having likeness or appreciation for a person can help us lighten up, while some of the more uncomfortable and deep conversations can allow us to know we care more than we used to. Being nervous can expand our capacity, though the lighter and happy points of likeness and love also are needed for our spirits.

If we're always in conflict and chaos, the stability of truth may not be known. It can distort ourselves and cause doubt, and as I had written about the three corners of love, trust, and appreciation in *Built from Within*, and I also found that I've used the word love a lot; 56 times up to now in this book.

When editing of *The Sands of Yesterday*, I found that I had obsessively used some words in that work also. The words 'also' and 'too' are overused by myself in the diction that I use. I use the words to add additional ideas, yet I value diversity in language and sometimes haven't shown it.

I remind us that it's not only me in these books. They include many links, associations, and mental chimes that tell me I feel sad about how it is. Knowing love can deepen a person's capacity for empathy, sadness, and understanding, and deep self-investigation will find more of our internal faults. The wonders and worlds help us discover the interactions and involvement with others.

This process is not an easy thing, though it will develop our comprehension of integrated life. I understand I have lapses of emotional capacity and don't quit even know how it is to be another person. I feel empathetic sometimes, yet have had a lack of sympathy in some cases. Each of us is a different person in physical form, yet our spirits, hearts, and souls mingle and interact; as making our minds.

A capacity of experience will expand our comprehension,

and often the fear of involvement may cause me to disband or disengage. REMEMBER TO BREATHE!! Take another breath. Rhymes may confuse the impulse, yet we emulsify the stars shed for the tears and bars wed to how it mustn't be said.

We shall not mislead or be misled.

Separation from some is a good idea. Some wish to push the limits and abilities. Uncomfortability can aid in personal growth, and I believe in growth too. Each day we have a chance for an intentional choice to do so.

Each day forms by a sequence of events that were mostly held in control, even if not our own. I don't like to exert or try to control others, and I also don't enjoy being controlled. Some may say to surrender and release the reigns of control, yet *self-control* is a value I hold.

I prefer to be responsive, not reactive, as I like to choose how to respond and not be forced into decisions. I told you, I don't want to act. I learn more of my values each day and have a deepening and widening of my understandings and capacity. The problematic days may still be good days; they are days of growth and expansion.

Schweppes Cranberry Raspberry Ginger Ale was my drink when I wrote the base of this chapter. I had two cans from a neighbour and was drinking the first of two. I crossed the over the reference to Jessy and the light effervescence of her attitude and personality. She's not a drink, though what an excellent way to start the day.

I also think of Glenna and how I wrote how she's like a glass of champagne. Then, with the drinks, I think of Lewis and green juice and how I haven't played his podcast recently. I also neglected a phone call with Greg and how I hoped him to be a coach in the New Year.

I still have a lot of work to do. I carry my parents, cousins, friends, community, and pets in my heart, my mind, my soul, and our future. It was the night of December 15th and 16th, 2017 at this point. School completed for the semester, and there was one Snowpeaks meeting for that year. I aspired, wished, hoped, and prayed to go to Vancouver airport. I went.

I'm thankful that I'm allowed to know and interact with so many different people, and if we rewind to chapter two of this book, the premise of bonding is accurate. It may be that I've been fused and welded to some, yet the truth also is that I may not be stable as liquid or gas. Plasma is a thing, though, and the conspiracies may wish I not be a spirit.

With the plan and plot in mind, let us wind up into 2025 a bit sooner than expected, and push the build date for 2023. I think we can do that; that said, an idea from Magic. I hope my converted mana cost five, so I can share three points of mana.

That converted mana cost idea also stems from my fear of a Fatal Push, yet I recall that that card only targets creatures. I can still be a Mox, yet must watch out for artifact destruction. I don't know what decks they're playing, or what cards they have as the metagame of Earth is elaborate. I lack knowledge and still must learn far more so that we may plant the seeds.

I'm reminded to not think too far in the future though am plotting and planning for how to live life. It must be formed with others, and not just by my wishes and wants. We share growth, and it's not only individuals or singular people that allow our futures; we are all part of the great chain.

We also may be the seeds of life individually, though we aren't only plants. We each are living organisms with nodes of perception, consciousness, and experience. We may bond and interact, though we also are not simple elements that hold clear and constant similarities. We may stream and flow, yet the pathways of life we walk decades later may not yet exist in our awareness.

Many wish for permanency, yet the moment of when is now. There are wishes, wants, and even prayers for the future and past, yet the most actual moment we have access to be the present. I could be wrong about that.

When we are in our thoughts, we are there, precisely in the world, and when we are awake, we are there, apparently not living in a dream. Still, the realms of visions on Earth are real; they are vivid, they are, also in our beings, explicitly ours to know. Déjà vu can share how some are living a dream.

If you can remember a dream or the past, no one else can experience or see that the exact way that you do; that is yours to know. Your memories or experiences may not be understood or comprehended by another; it is also just your point of view. It's best not to say we know or fathom others dreams; we have never lived their life, and we have not been who they are. We've not had the relationships or interactions with other people the way they have. We sometimes cannot know even how to believe we understand due to extreme distortions. Is that where that famous saying arises again?

"Know thy self."-Socrates

Is this where we should say we don't know; because it's not us? I must not make claims, beliefs, or assumptions as to what another's truth is. I have never lived their life, and I have never walked a thousand years of time to be there next to them. I cannot claim to know; I must not presume that I have a clue, and I see that I don't know.

I am not one to write or solve mysteries. I am meant to live, learn, and experience life, and then use it as a conduit to help form, cultivate, and strengthen just and stable lives. The purpose of my work is to provide, yet my function is not purely monetary. I need to remember that I can help other's lives by tending to the gardens and *also* by plowing in the fields.

We work together, even if we are not are all the same.

IN FAITH OF OUR TRUTH

1:21 AM December 21st, 2017. It had been a super-trippy night. I was working on putting *Fragments of Intent* online, and a message from an ultra-positive friend that I don't entirely know sent me a note that deeply concerned me. Their message inclined the belief that the world was going to go to chaos and we should prepare for a full disconnection from 'the grid.'

I was frightened, and it carried me through some other parts of my cowardice. I know I pray to God, and I also am terrified not only of what happens on a global scale, though even on a cosmological level. I work for the Kingdom of God, though I cannot claim that I want to fight.

As I was deep editing *The Sands of Yesterday* I glimpsed awareness of the Creator. I work in different ways than most, and I also understand I'm explicitly a vassal and not one in control. That causes me to fear too. I know that I'm not one who has power and I have concerns about the forces on Earth.

Even if I were asked to be a primary leader for a great many people, I don't think I would want such a responsibility. I serve people, I don't rule, though I write and record. I work for many more than a few, and I also know I would prefer to provide for many than be part of a battle.

Though my lack of knowledge is extreme, I put my faith and wishes to the higher powers of the Universe. I have an intense fear that my loyalty to God, His Son, and the Spirit might not convey I also have a desire to honour other forces of life including differing religions. That is where I see my weakness. I deem that my faith in God might upset some who don't believe in Him, and I fear condemnation for my belief system.

I wish to learn more about other religions as they are all part of Earth. Earth is where we are, and though we need to help all people, a difference of religious beliefs is part of the conflict I'm concerned about on this planet. Forces such as famine and wars over resources and power are also issues that I cannot resolve from my solitary point of a wish; Peace in every nation, Love for every race, Unity of every creed, and Respect for every religion. Global PLUR.

I know *I* must keep right with all forces of life, and I'm not sure how to address and meet people's needs with the levels of experience I have. Alone, I cannot assure world peace, though I have an idea that love is a vital and profound way to achieve it. When I find myself apart, I can wish for the worlds of life (not just Earth) to harmonize and bring about a unity of kindness, compassion, and grace for all people, yet it requires a collective commitment.

Some people on Earth are deplorable and have committed heinous crimes. Many things and actions have happened that I wish could be undone and never even be a thought. The thing is, I'm just one person. Peace and Love are fantastic, though we need the Unity of all and the basic instinct and action of full Respect to pervade.

Love can help seal Peace and protect lives, yet I don't know how we can ensure lives are kept safe. If people collaborate in, with, and for PLUR, I still feel like a fool and wishful pansy for wanting there to be love and not war.

It was near Christmas day when I wrote this. The previous year I was at the home of appreciated friends for Christmas and was writing *Searching for Tomorrow*, the 2nd Fountain book. So much has happened since then, and the ideas of hope, security, and truth draw more thoroughly now.

From my heart of wishing and praying, God, please allow us to live. Please enable goodness to thrive, please let peace expand, and please let unity fortify each person's bonds of faith. Please permit us to respect, please grant us forgiveness and our needs, and allow the world to understand Earth is a combined responsibility.

I cannot fathom the consequences of my life let alone the weight and severe complexity of what Earth is as a whole. I have a very narrow comprehension and wonder if 'keeping in my lane' is neglecting cues from the Universe to aid and tend other lives.

I am sorry for not understanding God and the world, yet He is one I honour with heart, mind, body, soul, and spirit, even if I don't know what the plan is. I fear what some may want to do to Earth, yet there are many issues in other countries that I don't understand. There also are fantastic people that work for, in, and with PLUR, even if not known by that name.

I have a strange human point of view that reminds me that Earth is not the only planet that holds life. I've not yet known about the intents of life outside of Earth's atmosphere, though my faith calls me to intuit we are with them also. My wishes to the Universe are not only shared with Earth; my intentions on this planet are out there in other parts of the Universe.

In our solar system, the scientists have not confirmed life on any other planets or moons. I dare not say some things directly to God due to an extreme reverence for Him. Because of this chapter's title, I add the word reverence as an R-word to PLU8R too.

For the humans that read this, I wrote about PLU8R (with an 8) in the chapter *A Brief Trickle of Insight* in *The Sands of Yesterday*. My understanding is that God is one of the most critical and central parts of things, though I cannot often share my perceptions or awareness of God. Each must find their own belief and knowledge of who guides us and how.

For myself, I know that primal, rational, and simplistic forces guide me. The primal part is my non-God intuition and my psychic and social paranoia. I was diagnosed as a paranoid delusional schizophrenic in 1998 and also went through excessive drug use. Two decades later I'm highly aware and sometimes fearful of even the slightest noise or shift of energy or thought.

Direct command rarely guides me; I rarely am told what to do, and even when I request guidance, sometimes I don't act. Some things that cue me to action, I do some things I know are not good, and intuition plays a substantial role in my life. I hold drastic homage for some I don't yet comprehend, and my instinct and impulsive obsessions base fragments of thought. My ideas slip upon time moving through parts of the maze I travel.

The regarding of cognitive forces strongly link my mental grounding points. My Earthly father is exceptionally rational and guides me with hope and also choiceful advice. I've not heeded him so often, though he also brings me 'back down to Earth' sometimes. My Dad has a solid belief and trust in life, and even if not one who's religious or has a belief in God, he knows how to love me.

I've not often acted on or heeded good advice usually or adequately. I need to sleep more regular hours, yet there it was at 2:18 AM convinced I need to complete my work at the expense of sleep and chemicals. I know people that would urge me not to stay up late, and cigarettes and coffee may be entirely blasphemous as an idea to some.

My Dad, though, is the one on the planet that I trust the most. He lives overseas and is thoroughly loving, caring, and supportive. Even if he can be critical, my Dad has learned how to love me unconditionally as I make my follies and failures in earning my own life.

When I wanted to sell music and make a career from my recordings, he told me that I'd need to be 'really really lucky,' and I still think that I am. Even though I've not sold many copies of my books yet either, my Dad encourages me to create while also urging me to form more positive choices. I am exceptionally thankful to like and love my Dad, and in January

2018, I got to spend 18-20 days with him and his wife at their home.

I adore Australia trips! They are so drastically peaceful and enjoyable! I get to spend time with two amazing people, my Dad and Sarah and also have luxuries of feeling safe and separated from the chaos, calamity, and fear of my own life in Chilliwack.

I get to see my Dad about once every two years, and paranoia sometimes hounds me the few weeks before going to visit. That happened with the most recent trip to Australia. With the extreme fears and paranoias I felt in my body summer 2017, and the months after, it was beyond my comprehension about how good it would feel to be there at their home.

December 27th, 2017. I won't track all of what happened, yet to and for the future we go. In the inscription of my review copy of *The Sands of Yesterday*, I wrote: "Keep true & let the sands of time form the consecrations of True, FS & TGH." These three things are things for which I work.

True, with a capitalized T, is my reference to Natalie. I still wish to meet her, though and I also know that she is probably best to not be with me. FS is Full Seed which is the Providing Point objective to reach its big hairy audacious goal of providing 250,000 shelters and 10,000,000 people with water. TGH is The Glass House, a home I've envisioned.

The three goals are guideposts for my future. Regarding Natalie, she is a teacher and tethered to my being, and though my written work started with her in mind, she is still loved even if I can't be with her. Full Seed is what I wish the results of my work shall be, and as a focal point of thinking, the three things include many things and people.

Earth is within the global and local communities, and up to December 2017, I had yet to sprout into action. The life force that holds fast my commitments to earn my materialistic wants and prosperity are harboured with a function for others also.

A personal objective is to provide $15,128 for up to 1,000 people. If I can do so and follow through with the idea to earn like the 1% and share 99% of it, I make $15.28 million a year my income will be $152,808. Far more than I need.

The Glass House is a contialitic centre for others. By using the amount needed for one year of mortgage payments, I then divided by 25 to find out how much it will cost per session to provide the home payments with 25 gatherings.

After compounding the math, the presumption includes covering other living costs and not just the mortgage. I'll write in the future about these sessions, though for now, the premise to share is how to reverse the math.

When we know how much something will cost us, we then can know what we are working towards. If it will cost me $8,000 for a car and I want to have $1,500 for one year of insurance, that's $9,500. I instead round to a greater number of $10,000 for a car. We then can divide $10,000 by $5, $10, or $20 units towards the total. 2,000x $5 notes, 1,000x $10 notes, or 500x $20 notes will be needed to provide for my next vehicle.

This chapter has squirrelled from the initial fears I held when starting it. One week of time can drastically shift a point of view and infuse a considerable shift in attitude. A week ago, I was afraid for the life of the planet, and today I've gone back into self-study and plotting and planning future numbers for my goals. Natalie started my process, yet I hope she understands that my work is far more than where the first book began.

Perchance I have an overly active desire to accomplish things, and also have displayed sloth. The point that reels me back in is giving and how I'd shared promises of prosperity for others without yet securing my situation. Awareness though! We must dream massive dreams, be aware of where we are, and then move forward to get to those dreams.

The revision and editing process is not one that I'm always thoroughly fond of doing. It feels like I'm slowly trudging through the mud and not generating what we require for Full Seed. I do know that the books must be available for sale if there are going to be sales. The 'one step at a time' and 'there are no shortcuts' notions are true points, yet it's also true I feel guilt grasping at my being for not yet providing. The distant dreams and fields are on the horizon, and I also wish I could teleport people to where they want to be.

I'm glad to take a break once in a while. If you find yourself at your plow, as I have been with my bookwork, it is okay to lift the plow and get into a different field. I shifted like that today by pausing the audiobook I was playing for the hours I devoted to editing and came back to this book. I plant more in this garden and field while maintaining that I also don't stop short or quit.

Remember, you can pause or shift to other ideas, work, or activity, just be sure to complete what you started and said you are going to do.

With Full Seed, there is a time issue. When I was writing the 3rd and 4th Fountains, my goal was 15,000 books sold by August 1st, 2017. I didn't reach that goal. Not even close! I did though refuse to give up and quit. I keep active with my bookwork and implement perseverance. A Magic poster at a local card shop holds the words "We shall endure."

I feel a bit of shame for not providing more, though that unease also urges me forth and assists my will to make sure I keep moving forward. Having a dissatisfied feeling about something can call a person to action. Making commitments to do things can assuage that feeling and alleviate our unease.

I've gotten obsessed with a few things that nibble at my innards, and my discomfort compels me to keep at it. Uncomfortable feelings can be a motivation to cause change, though remember to maintain your integrity and values held fast when you act.

Respect yourself and remember that courtesy is not as common as we may like it to be. That is where you too must fortify your spirit, beliefs, and actions for strengthening what is right and just. Honour yourself by allowing your dreams to adjust how you approach life. There must be faith in the process and the work we each have is different than others. I pray well you are committed to yours. I must remember I keep the plow in the fields for yields of the cosmos.

Thank you for allowing us this journey and for letting me heed my inner guidance. I still have a great deal to learn and develop, and I'm appreciative of the others who help this. I remind myself there is still much to accomplish.

PLOTTING AND PLANNING

I've mentioned before that the term 'the plan and the plot' are the positive and negative conspiracies. For my sanity, I must grip the terms and wrestle them into what I may do. After a week of going to bed earlier (other than Christmas Night), I'd not stayed up late to write, though on December 28th, 2017, I felt compelled at 10 PM to put a plan on paper.

On February 5th, 2018 I was to put on a Kickstarter campaign online that would run until February 19th. On December 28th, I was laying down to go to bed, though found a thought and got up to get my Introversial journal. In that book, I wrote some ideas and points about the Kickstarter campaign. I then felt the urge to get to the desktop computer to extrapolate the ideas and share them in this book.

As one of the reward items for the campaign, people were to receive a copy of this book in printed form. I want to share with others the process of my plotting and planning.

First, there was the idea to Kickstart a campaign. I had done so with *Fragments of Intent* in February 2017. We had not reached the $2,000 goal, though did receive $719 in pledges from 16x backers. Since running that campaign, I learned some lessons about how to run a Kickstarter more effectively in the future.

One primary thing I didn't do with the first campaign was

to market before the starting date. People didn't know about the Kickstarter until the day I had put it up online. From not pre-marketing, the campaign didn't get immediate traction and display early results to encourage future backers. I know now to give advanced notice for the next Kickstarter if I'm to run another. I chose not to run the 2018 Kickstarter in February.

If you are reading this book, many hurdles and challenges have been overcome to allow it to be. Both *The Sands of Yesterday* and *Fragments of Intent* have gone through numerous revisions and are higher quality books that I would have been able to provide for the 2017 or 2018 campaigns. Dare I even spin forward into the future when this book combines into its three-part compilation? The advice, though, is one step at a time.

Because I'm not there yet, I can't predict future outcomes, yet plotting and planning can help influence a result. Just like how the plots and plans others doesn't mean there will be a success, to have an idea is vital.

What I'd like to do with this process is to pass through it and arrive with full funding. I'm reminded of the broader goals outside of the bookwork, though also see it as a crucial point. For the long-term, getting books into people's hands will share the ideas and expand them.

When I first formed this text, I hadn't even yet received the first review of any of my books on Amazon. I also hadn't sold the first store copy through Ingram. The determination to continue has kept a lot of this going, and I also know it just feels right, even if I've not received monetary success to this point.

On January 7th, I went to Australia to visit my Dad and Sarah and returned on the 26th-27th. I planned to use my creative time there to run the Kickstarter yet set it aside to enjoy a holiday. I didn't want to chain myself to a process such as actualizing a campaign when on holiday. If the Kickstarter is only one point or activity in a grander scale of time and work, then I must also think of a more distant horizon of ideas. Later on, I didn't realize it was a definite idea to run it.

My understanding of the need to realize Full Seed is crisp. I'm aware that each day the books aren't selling that people are going without a home, and without many pledges via Patreon, it doesn't feel right. How do we reach Full Seed locally? I'm obsessed with this! It's not a positive feeling.

My books *are* a tool that can be used for the local community, though I too must put in additional effort into networking and securing other supports for people. Advocacy and education are helpful, though I admit I've not been close to the problems people face. I have been in my creative process and worked instead of marketing and generating sales, or even garnering pledges.

I could use the excuse that the books aren't yet in final form, though I twist back to a weird faith that I *am* doing a lot of the 'right' things. I did push for an early release for review copies of *The Sands of Yesterday*, and I also put *Fragments of Intent* online with Ingram in 2017. This glacial pace seems to daunt my hope because of a shown lack of results.

If the Kickstarter campaign were to succeed, it would mean that more copies of the books would be out there in the world. Those books, though, are not significant income sources for Providing Point yet. Even if I can order copies, they need to be sold to generate income. It is forward movement, though so minor compared to the total situation and needs there are to house everyone.

It's even far more profitable for Providing Point to sell Amazon copies, as the 51% of the earnings go towards helping others, though what about awareness and exposure? My understanding of the tiny size of the local market is what causes me to think we need to expand the books outside of Chilliwack.

Here's some more math; if *one in a million* people buy a book from Amazon, then $3.22x7,000=$22,540. With the recalculation of how much it will be for Full Seed, that's not even two individual's Yearly Seed. If we provide 1,000 Yearly Seeds, that will mean we'll need to sell 4.7 million books alone!?

When I use a massive goal and rewind the numbers to the

finite points of what we can provide, it seems to shift me to a lack and fear-based point of view. I also, though, was told that the numbers need to be used and processed to find our solutions. What, then, if we can get one in ten thousand people to buy a copy? That's near 149 Yearly Seeds. Potential nudges my mind back to the idea of collective input and not just the work of one kid and his books.

Guidance from online mentors and influencers talk about passive income and multiple streams of income. I understand part of that now. Once we complete a book or album and make it available online, it can stand on its own to earn in the future; that's passive income. Having numerous books or records also encourage additional sales; that's multiple streams.

Though the music and books need to be distributed and purchased, the work of making them is the investment given. If I have one product and sell 100,000 copies, it's like having ten products and selling 10,000 copies of each. If there are 100,000 customers, what if they buy all ten products? That's a million sales.

I don't want to taint the numbers, yet spin that down a few zeros to relay a point of information. Would you like to sell one thing to ten people, or ten things to one person for the same result? It may seem more difficult to sell all ten items to just one person, though what if you sell one product to ten different people, they like what you've sold them, and you have ten other things they want to buy too?

If you only have one thing to sell, then you need to play more of a numbers game. If you hold many things that you can sell, when the customers like that thing and want to buy more or your products, it'll be beneficial to have other products. Some also advocate selling the items for a higher price for higher earnings.

In the creative space, I'd like to have much available for others so that those enthralled with what I make share and wish to have more. The more items, products, or works I have available for them, the higher the chance for more sales.

When I was forming this book, a challenge was how to get

books in front of eyes. My music is online, yet I must heed and check in with myself if I'd like to be on phones or stereos.

Some people excel at making many things like a factory and have a vast quantity of product for the sake of the product. Some other people will focus and hone and craft one piece obsessively without completion. We can say there is a third type of person; one who produces high or fantastic quality things, and *also* many of those things!

That's where I'd like to be with my work. My books are improving in quality as I form them, and we've gone through the revision process together with some of them. With the lessons and experiences I've had writing books, there also has been a vast difference in how and what I produce. I'd like to improve further the quality of what I've written, formed, and developed by creating more, yet also assure that I'm building a valuable quality product that will be worthwhile for readers.

The add-in of honing one's craft and putting in the creative reps is a thing I adhere to in fact. I hope others also think of the purpose of what they're doing and why they're doing it. My situation is basic. I recorded a lot, I didn't get a super-positive financial response, so I shifted to other pathways of creation. My activities hadn't yet earned an income, though I didn't give up.

If one thing isn't working for you, then it *is* an idea to try something different. The different work or activities don't need to be out of the field you're working, though, as it's sometimes beneficial to link ideas, projects, and skills.

My whats and whys have changed drastically since the first time I pressed 'record' on the stereo. When I first recorded, my intent was to get signed to a record label for $250,000 and marry Demma, a girlfriend in the Philippines. When I started writing my first book, I wanted to use the book to meet Natalie. It was 'the girl' that called my creativity.

Why do I like to make things? Why am I up late at night writing these books? Why do I refuse to quit? Because I have things to share and have committed to earning a living. I also shifted to creating for others so I can benefit people other than myself. Although not as much in the *Etched in Stone* part of *Shards of my Soul*, the Fountains evolve into valuable information that others may use in their lives too.

I'm committed this process even if I think I'm many years away from meeting some of my objectives. When we form a book, there can be a target audience, and it's best to know the main lessons or suggestions are for that audience.

I haven't written that way up to now, though I'm learning. It's part of my 'how,' and it's taken me a few many years to know some of my whys and whats. As mentioned, though, we also learn through mistakes, experimentation, and change.

Because some whys and whats aren't static, the ways I add value to people is by opening myself up to the Universe, life, and experiences after failing, stumbling, and sometimes by folly. I then report to others what happened to me. I am a valuable open book, though I'm even more valuable as a person to talk with about life, plans, and connections.

I see this as it forms and feel thankful I'm learning how to provide and create. My intents are many, and as we fuse our experiences into the moment of 'when' we reach awareness, I wish, hope, and pray, that we all gain.

Writing *is* a thing of faith. When I type out to anyone or even a specific person, that's me telling them or the Universe what I want to say to them. When I write to people openly about my life, and they learn *their* lessons by seeing how I guide, that's a form of knowledge we share.

My wishes, prayers, and hopes align the sequences of awareness as we channel these series of text that I honestly didn't how would meet this point is where unclear antecedents mix. She didn't know what she wants to do, and me not knowing her or why we're doing what we do reminds me of how You are not True. How can we intend who we are as part of all three points beyond the light?

The when and where meld this too. It's our temporal and locative positions of mind, body, spirit, soul, and heart as we blend together. Who we are, where we are, and anytime we're aware in the 'now,' we are being guided explicitly by fate.

What do I want?
I want to thrive.

Why do I want it?
I love to live.

How shall I live?
By providing for the worlds.

For whom shall I provide?
Those who want and need.

What shall I provide?
Some seeds of life for a multitude.

I analyze myself as I form this. I clarify how I can state my points clearly, though I think it's to live. The thoughts provide life, and I've had a resonant fear that I'm not entirely producing enough for people. I've thought people are upset that I've not earned for them either.

The love of being alive has me fixed upon thinking I need to provide proof for others to allow myself my own life. What happens if I shift the order of the five questions? If I change what people want is that me forcing the release of control.

What if what God wants is also what we want? Would ideas lean to think that if we're still alive now, that it's something in His accord? What for those that don't have a religious or spiritual faith? What of those who've passed on already? What can I tell them?

I don't have insight into what I need to do sometimes. I also must explicitly say I don't know how all things meld. Fear *has* commanded me at points. I'd prefer to learn through love.

Reverence is included as an R of PLU8R, though it's a word I now think need not be entirely religious. Respect based on authority or high honour with love can solidify. My Freedom Solution includes being free of fear, though yes, God, thanks for allowing me to live and fortify reverence for life.

For those who aren't religious, you may think I'm a delusional or misguided fool; we can't yet fully know. When I get focused on God, my creativity almost freezes. I have felt insignificant and that it's best my efforts are not for achievements. I've written a lot while in solitude, and wonder how to live with another person. I think living with another cat could be radical, though how would that change my situation?

At the end of the moment of now, the plow holds in the dirt. Skirting the issues is a different thing altogether as I'm concerned that my why is also based on the way I want to live and that, in many ways, it's not something I hold entirely in my control. Self-responsibility is a thing, though I also mustn't bribe or make false promises. I have made many proclamations, and the fact that I've yet to fulfill them concerns me. I don't like how so much is still floating in the air, yet also am glad there are signals, signs, and warnings.

Though I've heard I'm the only one who can control my actions; I know that may be untrue. I do though accept responsibility for my choices. What I also need to trust is those who are for myself resist the manipulation of my being. If trust, stability, integrity, self-control, and loyalty are five of my success indicators, then I must fortify them and also be open to experience and learning. I also must allow myself to accept I'm alive for reasons not yet known to me.

I'd like others to find themselves active, sheltered, warm, safe, and well too. How we build in the future has yet to be known, yet I also must not rest upon the promise of Seed. I thank You, I appreciate the readers, and I also ask we may be alive and well decades from now.

I've not seen the future, I'm not a prophet, and I also hope we can earn a profit. These books are my pathway to my Freedom Solution, and though I often am without another human in my home when they form, I hope that another feline friend can land here within the next three months. I'll let you know their name if they do.

ANOTHER ROW OF SEED

These grains left along the shoreline; some are sand, and some are seed. They carry signs that the net opens up to find us dropping in on the vertical ramp to skip the lines. Though they may spell me to occur, the mental burrs picked up the trough.

A scoff of good drink should link how I nudge her forward with what we think. I heard the brink of what to connect, yet I can't select her farms and share how the phones and alarms remind the clones of her charms. I dare not think to puff the bluff of my shards while guards hold the pup up. I think of how it will be to sup with Ibuki in the cup.

Red XIII has linked the lines off the stage while signs remind Hope and Paige that their Mom will always love. The blur finds the cure of time shares the rhyme into how we climb into the pit to sit down and nestle up. Even if it is with water, our daughter, a potter, cannot foretell the Shell and how they now dwell in the text.

Directions shift a gift to lift out a doubt from some that sprout. I can tell you about many things, yet it's best we speak and not be deceived by a mental leak. They peek into the fold of how I'm only one that the Valley's controlled.

I accept you. I request True. I'm opening to renew that my questions answer the crew. Affections of connections shift my verbal directions into how I can say "I love you" to many yet not so much those that wish me death. Beth was her name, yet we know that it's the moments of time I now claim to know.

Hold a symbiosis in the way you help me to show us what is fact by touch. Much holds the charts, and though my hearts open and closed to the doors of how I proposed; I also ask myself, be fully exposed. We each are what matters, yet I think I cannot plan the plot as the spell scatters.

The plans of the worlds beyond Earth remind me that I'm in the fabric of our thoughts. It's not just that my Dad that tells me not to think of her; another in PLU8R keeps the sands of sleep deep in the spirit that's wept. I kept myself aside from the world, while some have me curled up and away. I almost always think to say I still don't know I think I can convey.

You may not betray my truth, yet find the fields of our youth as I'm a dogged and ragged son. It's reminded us that some webs are not spun to catch yields of prey, yet instead to have a safe place where our soul may pray. Come into forever for today to remind why I try to hear myself say; that they may tell me things I have yet to learn how to play.

You know I have hoped, wished, and prayed that a real meeting would relay, yet I still seem to cast the spade in the Earth. I urge myself to forget that I could even hold a shard of worth, yet birth comes from a perspective that life is more than the Primary Directive. George keeps the sieve of how we live on the same planet, and that gives me just a glimmer of hope.

I must remember in this instant, that if I do love, I could call this instant the wall. There is a split between now and then that keeps me with the plow. I love you too, Dad, though your son still carries decades of loss with her as a cross.

I'd like to meet my lovestone, even though I think she wants me to leave free the key and never think of holding her as an Underground Sea. I mean not the games of Rap and Hip-Hop, or even House or Trance, yet instead how what we speak starts the chance of the delicate social dance.

The Underground Sea reference is how we make this Dimir.

We find the apparent layers of players who refuse to give into how I feel I may never live, yet I cannot say it to your face. I also know that our spirit shall never replace how God has given us grace while it seems I trace the decades lost because I was terrified I was the one who'd pay the cost.

I tossed aside the tossing to guide, yet I know I cannot reside in a tide of DNA. It may let me say what I mean to those who allow me to do what I do. I can't tell True on the phone a way to be known, yet by the tones of our thought, the zones of what it is not.

Likely the way I hone in on the spin is that, with me, Cupid never made a sin. You are the one I cherish, even if seeing you is what you crave I never need. I think that I have so much less than a guess, that they bless each foretold keystroke I cannot hold. There is much control for me to know that will forever keep the fold.

Let the lines fall away into how I wish you hope and pray. There is a way for us to nestle in our beings without being trapped, shackled, or chained. I am not God. I am not a judge. I'm a sod whom you know wishes that he could budge from his position of how he knows she can never be my only mission.

I don't build my fantasies alone. I clone and condone them to be something that is together seeded and grown. Even if I cower and hide behind the fact of opening up my entire being to us as your guide, I don't think you trust or love me in the ways your tears have yet cried.

I have obsessed and over-focused to best not claim I'm right, correct, or just. I too wish not to declare my words as something I must. My wishes are like Petri dishes that hold a diverse network of whims and wants.

Some ideas I've written, though, are not just fantasy. They are parts of life that have etched into my being like a stone. It would take lifetimes to pass before some of the stains in my heart could be cleared, and that's just the surface.

Shall I expose my depths of my being in these books? It seems like a safe place. No one's reading them anyways. I've handed out or sold hundreds of CDs and 150+ books and have barely heard a thing from anyone. The devotion to the editing process and my dismal attempt at marketing and distribution seems like a complete waste of time. I have not 'found' Natalie. I have not yet 'searched' for tomorrow. If I am the Fountain, then why don't I hear from the Valley.

The seeds haven't yet grown, and the fields have been left untended. I see no glimmer near or far, and I can't even claim to have a stone with whom to etch together into your fate. If I am clay, it seems few wishes mould me in a stable silty puddle. It seems I have tried to build a house upon the sand.

I have no rings of Saturn orbiting my heart and soul to stand correctly. Of being grand or great? I'm a fool. I am not cool. I am not a jewel. I am not them or You or True. I'm not even a two, and I can only now wish that I know, for now; I am beyond the understanding of five, four, and three as crew.

I set free from the path of pursuit and involute myself into a point of being that can see into the bits and bytes of all the lost who left the rights. I've not thrown a hook. I've not layered correctly to have sifted the soil in a way that will not let the sediments roil into your book.

I stand upon the natural foreign ground where the Heavens resound the truth wound into the sound. Although I surround myself with none, the signals from the sun tell the son to move into how there is much I prove. The grooves of the disk reflect the consect and direct my life to not to need to call for action.

"It seems like it'll always be a whole number if I'm at the bottom of a fraction."

There will always be many above me, yet the base idea is that none of you will ever understand or know what it's like to be me; just as I have near no clue as to what it's like to be you.

Natalie, do what you do. The complete vacuousness of my awareness of who you are and what you want is not healthy for either of us. It's ruining you emotionally, mentally, and spiritually. I feel ruined socially, physically, and financially.

The point of my life's journey is not one that I want to close with death before you, yet we meet and take a seat. Even if it means you to repeat that you hate me, the sacred tree carries our worlds into the oceans and the sea.

She may want me to never even think of you, and may never consider being in the same room as me for five minutes, let alone an hour. It would be a gift of great compassion to tell us those things. You saved souls from an eternity of never knowing, and also can potentially protect yourself from decades of degradation and or dead dream from your wishes.

These have been centuries of love, even if it is entirely one-sided. I have given love a bad name because I don't know what it's like to love another as the same. I'm clouded with smokes and ridicule, and I disparaged you and myself with my obsession. Ultimately, it could all stop quite quickly by making contact to remove my decades of never knowing.

It doesn't matter what I think or felt about you, it seems, and I also can't continue as I am. I will not play a power card over another or you, though maybe I have by writing this. The writing reminds me of how it seems I am one who never seems to understand the world of Earth orbiting the sun.

I've heard it doesn't matter what another tells me I should do, that I should follow my heart. You should follow your heart too. There may be a reason you've never heard from me, and I wish you know I know you cry. I cannot cross any of the purposes of why into why I also shy away from the day where there is air to breathe and the chance to seethe in happiness.

Natalie was my depraved longing, and, yes, this is my foul, tainted self. I know I cannot correctly express or show or tell a tree not to be a tree. Tear all the leaves from it in winter, trim back all the nasty branches you don't like because the birds wish to build a nest, and poison its roots and tear them from the soil. Dare they even set the tree in a fire and dance around it in pure extasy or dismay? It still doesn't remove the fact that there was a specific tree of life that shed a seed that heeded its nature to land in the soil and sprout to grow.

We thrive to become that we've never been before. That tree may instead live and thrive. I am a seed that knows the forest existed and pervaded through time with rare particles of the universe that existed and exists forever. You cannot take the seed out of my heart. And so the sands of time pass through the hourglass as we scatter to the winds.

The tree is not forgotten. The soil remains true. The view across the landscape reminds me that I knew. I'm sorry for not putting my faith in more than just the Universe. It comes from the point of being that I may never see clearly in my mind that no matter where I go, they will wind up the fuels and splice jewels to my DNA.

The blend of what they say will never take the truth away. Forever and a day; it's a day that seems to be okay with forever to follow. Though forever starts tomorrow, and we search for it, the thing is, as soon as we get to tomorrow, it becomes today. Forever still has not been met; it keeps us away with and from every word that we think, write, pray, and say.

Maybe I should quit? Perhaps I can go back to listening and dreaming. I've told so many what I want and wish, and it does matter, though a grain of sand in the oyster of life finds its way. We are free to do anything worthwhile.

The Fountains of Faith were meant to speak of hope and truth, yet it's clear I haven't done so much with the things to which my imagined divinity clings. I would like to know why.

When a person is left alone to ruminate in their thoughts, with no additional 'live' input, they are set free into thoughts of imagination. Being isolated and alone isn't easy, yet if I'm to return to Australia, I'd like to go there with another live entity in a year or two.

I have gone crazy and outlandish having no one to show and give love to properly. Maybe Nat was the fixated point of my thoughts since I'd not yet learned how to love on my own. Even then, I can't give the real version of them a hug to share with them how much I loved them.

We can.

I paused there to hear the whisper. That's an idea to relay; if you need to express love, and don't have a real person to embrace or a pet to snuggle, give yourself a super strong hug.

Wrap your arms across your chest and grab your shoulders with your hands. Imagining giving someone, anyone, a hug and doing so to yourself is better than not being able to tell another that you love them.

I may not like myself sometimes, yet I also may not understand or trust God enough to love Him alone. I can give an imaginary hug to someone and tell them I love them, and hugs may be a hack or pathway to necessary human recovery. Sometimes, anything is better than nothing.

It's true I'm not you. It's also true you can never be me. Though the fates weave and intertwine the signs of life, there are the facts of what is. I can't always tell you what the truth is, and I don't have a full voice.

The choices let me wind the threads of the loom into the way rhyme's trip and play, yet the slips of chips remind us to pray. Lay down and relax in the facets of your truth. They tell us about how we're together far in the past of our youth.

Our journeys *are*, right now, at the last moment of our awareness, yet we move forward and through into the unfolding future. Our truth will shape hearts, though some parts of life nudge us forward to remind us to find our kind. I wind the view of another who is true beyond the violet hue into so many and so few who cue the doors of my dreams into how the teams of life unfold.

An ultra-bold stance reminds us to dance and share the romance with some who suggest us to come from the point of pure love. We must not cross out Heaven, and I thank them too for telling me that we've yet to meet. The ideas of life hold my mind to my heart like a cleat.

I accept various higher powers above me are not God, and I ask that we may find the thread of my life to honour them too. I've dreamed of some who help us come from a point that tells me I do have high respect for many that I've yet to meet. Even if I know I don't want to be one to keep people under my feet; I admit some dreams remind me of that treat of grace. My confusion has once in a while surrounded me here in this place with the file of a cross denial.

I thank them too, and obscurely, I shall pay homage to many and a few without explicitly saying who. Or maybe I shall say their names? The thing is, there are far many more that can tell a thinly placed focus on just one may claim the aim of the game. We have yet to see the yields of my work; we've however seeded that heeded by the lost finding, up to now, that so very few have read what I've written.

I must be patient. The thing is, though, I think I've been *too* patient. I have left many forces of life up to the Universe and have not clearly understood that I and my work are for good, and people *shall* consume the text. While I'm alive, I shall write, and tonight I must form the signs and sights we see with an urge to use to press the key.

CHOICES OF TIME

I'm explicitly not God. I'm not you either. I'm still placed delicately into the foray of how I'm not sure how I'll get through to May. Although I was in Australia when I wrote this, I seemed to remember I hadn't had enough faith.

The Universe reminds us of time and space that the rhymes might chase the signs into Spinal trines. Four holds one of the symptoms told. I must trust in a few that more explore control with a choice of voices to manage my tone.

A few months ago I had a dream where they told me I had a fatal disease. I felt to actively deny the lucid prognosis, though the signs of my awareness pointed that I honestly thought that I had nothing for which to live. My work, like many humans, is vital to me and who I am, and one of the things that I value the most.

My poor me attitude, though, has projected concerns because it seems my work doesn't matter to anyone else. Even if *I* find meaning in what I form, it seems the world of Earth has little to no value in what I've done up to now. The fears compound by me is also thinking I don't matter enough to myself. I believe that I must have value for others and that I can do so by plowing the *Fountains of Fortitude*.

I may have an approval complex. I don't seem to value myself, and I've been searching for meaning by the results and effects of generating a positive life. Since I've not yet earned money for others or myself (my neurotic belief is my value and purpose is to provide), I must find my meaning and reason for living in things other than resources.

I don't have a girlfriend, pet, or children as a living legacy to work towards at this point. For those that have a spouse, business, or children, they know they have a definite purpose. Since I don't yet have those things or have provided for anyone else, I seem to think I have no value or meaning.

I must muster my faith and will to live. I want to live a long and prosperous life, though I honestly think I've been living an extended and impoverished survival. My wants have been grand, though am I wanting too much?

At the beginning of this book, I wrote some of what I'm grateful to have. I am thankful, and perchance I need to remember more of those things to urge myself to continue. I'm not searching for acclamation, and I'm not even really searching for extreme or ridiculous wealth. I'm not also seeking fame, though I do see that if the ideas and intents of my work manifest, it's unquestionable my work will result in those things.

My dearly loved cousin Julianna gave me a notebook many years ago that had a quote I think of now. I don't recall the exact wording of the quote, though its premise reminds me that I need to write to survive. I don't mean the crafty lies and deceits to fool those who are plotting my demise, yet instead, now, how the base level of how I *need* to write and build a strong faith to thrive to allow us to live.

It was incredible, beautiful, and fantastic to visit Australia with my Dad and Sarah again! Though I thought back to Chilliwack and my life there, I hadn't yet built a life of love and happiness. I feared from my self-focused nature and not earning love and respect from people I don't know how to have fully loving and trusting relationships.

I too need love to survive, and I feel tiny amounts or awareness of it when I'm unconnected at home. I've learned to be on my own, though, and I've also learned to forgive and love a few people and believe it. One thing regarding the fear of having a terminal illness is that I don't ever want my Dad to be sad. My Mom too, though the parent I was able to give a hug to and say "I love you" with full confidence and meaning the day I wrote this chapter was my Dad.

I saw something of my Dad one or two days before that called a terror to my being; like a deep insight into him and his placement in life. He is one of the most amazing men I know, and I also feel oppositely terrified of the idea of him passing before I do. Love is a saddening thing to understand when there isn't a guarantee the other will be there in the future.

I want to use this chapter as a reminder to myself of some primary reasons to live so that I will have a super strong desire to live and build a long loving life. I need to gather my being so that I remain healthy and not contract the disease of which would keep me from being alive. I *need* to write to force and allow myself to live. I want to thrive, yet first I must live.

I need to keep some ideas away from these pages to assure that I don't taint the wishes and prayers against my love and life from manifesting. It's sometimes helpful to discuss our fears and fantasies, though some of them may be more likely to occur if printed solid in the written word. Have you heard the saying "we write our own lives"?

I shall reduce the number of cigarettes I smoke, and I do want to live. I'd like to be healthy and active so that I can be alive and well to proactively engage in life. Small incremental improvements shall compound to aid to the grit of life that I wish and desire.

I'm exceptionally thankful to know I love my Dad, and I also am happy to have apologized and acknowledged to my Mom the remorse I felt for being so harsh to her when she was raising me. I'll continue to learn how to love more, and I'll also learn how to treat others with more care and respect.

I hope you develop the ability to know, share, and receive love from others too. I had received a kind acknowledgement from a friend where they thanked me for being there for them. Thank you also, Ajani! Reminders can help bring us together.

A gratitude journal is also a tool I think to use again. When we attune ourselves to things we are happy or glad for, it can motivate us to earn and do more of those things. As I become aware of behaviours that cause me happiness or joy, I also know to perform more of those actions.

When I was growing up, my Mom had the saying "You need an attitude adjustment." This chapter *is* that adjustment to assure I am alive with you, Mom and Dad, when you're both eighty years old. I could also focus on the gratitude for things not yet occurred that are in the future. Hope is helpful, and faith can help us get there, yet the victory will be when we reach those moments of time we've hoped, prayed, and worked towards and meet them.

In two days before this, I thought about Aeris, Celest, and Paradox, names for three kids whom I've thought I'd be 'Dad.' I don't want to use my kids as a reason to live (as that would make them my legacy and not their own), though hoping to meet them in the future is something I can use as a positive thought and also as a conversation with my future lovestone, whoever she is.

Love *is* something I drastically need in my life, and it barely seems to be there in Chilliwack. I must cultivate life well enough to grow some more love, and the idea of a pet surfaces again. A pet may be a good idea as having a pet will give me an entity to squeeze my love into, and it will provide me with a purpose by having another living being to love in my home.

Diana Pazdera has been a great friend. In a conversation with her, I mentioned how I wouldn't smoke in my apartment for the sake of my next pet. She was surprised I cared about the welfare of a cat when I seemed entirely okay to ruin my health with cigarettes. I know this today; I care a lot more about other people and lives that I often have for myself.

Some say we can't love another before loving ourselves. If that's true, then how can I like so much for some and still riddle myself with self-hate behaviours? I shall learn to love and care for myself, yet it also draws me to write that pleasure is not always a self-love activity. Pleasing someone or something isn't us enjoying them, though it is closely associated. Delights for ourselves, like my smoking, can be a distraction from the displeasure of the life we're living. Those behaviours may be more of a vice.

Committing to something is another thing. Too many proclamations without supportive action can taint a person. I know this with myself. I have proclaimed Seed Fund and Providing Point ideas and commitments, yet because I've not yet actualized them, I've partly had a stemmed subvert depressive and submissive behaviour.

Another concept is to find positive and healthy pleasures and relish in those as they'll additionally bolster our health and vitality. As I commit to a long and healthy life, my hope is my desire to smoke will decline, and I'll willfully quit the habit and acquire some anti-vices.

Thank you for a living. Even if my audience is currently near non-existent and the books haven't sold so much, I thank you, readers, God, and the forces that be for allowing me to direct these books and words outwards from myself. Even if I feel like I'm only one, I know enough of myself that I'm learning new ideas and pathways.

My faith must not rely on just the layers of text and my process; it also is built by God and the Universe. I had catastrophized my prognosis, yet I also send wishes and prayers out to the world and works of Earth for our realms of past, present, and future. New beginnings need not always be made at the end of another's life or journey; sometimes they may be spontaneously generated.

Dear Lord, I thank you for setting the cross on the tapestry. I ask you to place me alive and well here in the place where I sit two more years from now. Even if my willful wishes of earned prosperity don't manifest, and Providing Point doesn't 'solve' the full Chilliwack situation, I ask you to please use myself to instill Your love through me into the lives of this planet. Please let me become aware that I need not die to form a legacy.

Please draw me forward into living for the benefit of all that will remind me that this fall into my self is a way to start my faith. I do have decades of love, life, and work to do here on Earth, so thank You. You know my heart is learning, yet please make it sincere, secure, bold, and healthy too. I wish not to accept things meekly, and instead ask we may bring love, compassion, and kindness to all.

Let us learn and have other treats to enjoy other than our vices, and let our families be kept healthy and happy. As a motive for me to use to assure that I earn in the future, please let us move past when Celest reaches her terrible twos.

Please keep me humble enough to remember I'm held true and on course without anyone needing to control or misguide me with force. Thank You for the fact that I'm not to make a pact with the grave or need to proclaim that a subversive wish is what You wish for me to save.

I am grateful, thankful, and glad for the truths You let me know, and I also thank the forces of Heaven for keeping us on Earth below. The lives that are not on Earth may not yet understand how much there is to know in one breath, let alone the entire planet, yet let me be a living conduit to let them know some of the information you have allowed me to acquire.

I wish not to bargain or plea, yet the reminders are that You are You and I am me. What is right and valid for a few may be the wishes of death, yet I also know our needs shift and change succeeding with the reminiscing of Seth.

Grazie sempre, Dio. Mi ricordi che anche tu sei amore. I also hope that love is not the *final* frontier. Amen.

11:31 AM Brisbane time, Friday, January 19th, 2018

The reminders are clear. I'm not sure, though, how to tell the world that the lingering timelines of life are something that intertwines my mind with hope. The desires each of us hold may be similar to basic human wishes, yet some others are openly unique. I'm thankful my Dad makes the time to speak, and that when I've needed to be alone, he's let me that too.

My Dad and I are different people and living separate lives, and the in-person contact points we so rarely have are cherished. Some don't have that chance or opportunity with their Dad. Dad, thank you for giving me space, grace, and an ability to be me.

I returned to Canada in one week. It was a fantastic trip, and I'm glad that some of my spiritual understanding has deepened, even if not entirely in a religious context. The visit holds memories I wish to seethe in my spirit many years in the future. The visit to K'Gari in Queensland Australia reminded me of my reverence for nature, and the trees on the island are carrying a force and energy I can still feel. Thank you, K'Gari for laying down in the waters and resting there in Australia.

The Fountains seem to be slowing. I have written more for other books, and by being away from Chilliwack, I've not been thinking great amounts of thought about Providing Point. From conversations on the trip, the most frequent advice or push is that I need to learn how to care and earn for myself first and not for others. I'm not in full agreement, as I still think I may do both.

I have not told those who tell me to earn for myself first that I must maintain my commitments stated in *A Distant Glimmer*. It is true I may have overpromised, yet my ethical stance is that when I commit, to follow through. I've not always demonstrated that, though, when given a chance to uphold my promises, I like to do so.

What is *Etched in Stone*? Is it my promises of what I shall do with my creative work and also the call to the community to work for our solution? Is it that dream girl will always be one I think of, yet I do not remain chained? Is it that I'm a fixture of Earth that knows billions of lives are all connected both directly and indirectly? Is it even that I shall keep moving forward and creating after seeing such little monetary success by writing and recording?

The wishes are the imprint upon the stone as something thrown out into time and space and allowed to nestle in the valley. Even if not known, it draws us together.

The lives back home in Chilliwack hold parameters of their own. I've kept in loose contact with a few people while on this trip, yet I also must fortify and strengthen the bonds of love, trust, and appreciation with many other people. I remind us our relationships are ones where we need to connect, and friendship with friends hold an edge of hope on my forehead that seems to push outwards to thrive. Fortitude is a decision. I choose to make it so.

As I cannot make calls or meet up with some people back home, another choice is to enjoy and discuss the work and plans for when there. I do this through conversations, and writing my books with clarity agrees I need to develop my garden too. I have been in the fields without tending to my own life, and when I'm there in Dad and Sarah's garden, I want to remember to let them also be loved and appreciated too.

Dad and Sarah, and Mom and Owen have helped me so exceptionally much, as I learn more about acceptance and actualization. It's nice to have ideas and hopes, yet it's true we plan that I must act upon those urges to succeed.

So while I'm here in the garden, I recall the seeds are worthy and helpful; they are good hearts that want to help me thrive. Even if seeded and foreign to my understanding, some are beautiful and bold in my garden. I hope this trip is one where I shall have just, exotic, and unique seeds to share when I get back home. I may not be clear of who I'll find as a gal back home, though as Florencia guides me, we need to put a bit of romance in our friendships and some more friendship into our romance.

Two primary gals back home know that. There has been so much fantasy and wishing, and I know it's difficult to have a meal with an empty dish.

CHOICES OF TRUTH

The evening I wrote this, my Dad went to karate, and I chose to stay at his place to write instead. It's a choice that drew me into writing this, the closing chapter of the 7th Fountain; the first Fountain of Fortitude.

It is dangerous to love someone so much. I know this cognitively, and add that it's even more dangerous when the person is alive. When I started my trip to Australia to visit Dad and Sarah, I was at an exceptionally different point of time and energy. When I first got there, I was happy to see my Dad and Sarah, though also felt I had nothing to live for back home.

My fears twist my urges into driving and thriving forward with determination. I was to write this chapter to you, Dad, though I also must close this book with a cognitive parameter I use with Fountains; by making plans and, yes, proclamations for the future.

In 96 hours, I was to be on the airplane on the way to Hong Kong back to Vancouver. I needed time to gather my thoughts and intents for the future. I chose to write, and it twanged in my stomach as I missed a chance to go to karate with Dad. I fear so strongly of making him sad or disappointed in any way that my insides twist up and cause me to cringe.

We know that once we make a choice, ethical and wise, or foolish and wrong, that we must follow through and make the best of the situation. I do. I also carry forward into the trips and adventure. I gather facts, create new pathways, and then choose the best decisions. As the Fountains have not yet had commercial success, I must reassess my plans for the future.

Though I have written books, they haven't earned sales. I must generate ideas and concepts that have monetary value if I'm to use authorship as my primary income. Though I know that, I treat the Fountains as my development books as a way to enjoy and track the journey.

I have the luxury of sharing a more personal story, and as I can form words and write with such creative freedom, you are right, I need to find income sources that are reliable and plentiful. You're appreciated and loved, yet I didn't display that as well as I wanted to on the January 2018 trip.

Lessons filter into my awareness, and as I form book work and music recordings, I've often thought of the Australia trips as creative endeavours. I also carry an awareness. Dad's now 70 years old and 20 years is not a long ways away. One month can hold a lot of time, yet for the long-term of building my home, and having 90th birthday parties for my parents in that home is creeping up to the moments of now.

As I've promised earnings to Providing Point, it's 51% of the profits from my books other than 100% profits from *Seeds of Tomorrow*. I think a primary lesson I learned on the Australia trip is that I've given much without caring for myself, while still building faith in the future.

In preparation for the first printed version of this book, I dearly thank Gary Vee, and you should thank him too. I've written that if I adjust my commitments, they must add and not detract. From Gary, I've learned a lot, though my work ethic is not evident. Gary teaches exceptionally well, and it's his 51%/49% recommendation, we build. Thank you, Gary. I send you massive amounts of love, luck, life, and repent the fact I'm still not yet a successful entrepreneur or business builder.

The idea for *The Fountains of Flourishing* happened then. I don't know if that will be the next three-part release or the one after that. We'll see as we fortify the future together with this process. For now, I keep the sands in line, and with formed faith, must draw from every yesterday to work towards the rings of Saturn.

I love how some people don't believe in telepathy, yet it's a cornerstone of my awareness. In Chilliwack, Christianity is a primary religion, while in Australia, the mystical natures stem from Aboriginal 'dream-time' and also the modern satellite system and even subvert technology and electricity.

I recorded a video of the Lorikeets for my social worker back home. The Lorikeets gather in the thousands in an area near where I was, and they are happily vocal birds. I like them a lot! Other birds, like the lorikeet guides in Australia, are abundant. Back home, the crows and the seagulls give guidance with the Canada geese sometimes frequenting the skies with their signals, signs, sights, and sounds.

I discover much about myself on these journies of creative communication and relationship. Needs, patterns, and requirements found lots of difficulties connecting with my Dad because he and I are very different people. The way we process, accept, and communicate, is not easy being an ocean apart. I may be both a bit overbearing and oppositely lax and distant, and where I like to talk a lot about near anything, I note my Dad prefers to speak with more purpose.

I sometimes obsess about having a conversation, and also fear (a projected belief) that I may cause my Dad or others sadness for spending so much time on my own focused on work and ciggies. I love my Dad, though I also know he loves me. The fact I have a radical and excellent father is a blessing and treasure I cherish.

I may not show others so clearly how much I love them, yet that rewinds to how it's dangerous to care for someone so much. Love also can fortify a person's life here in present-day Earth to be around for another few decades.

I see a thread through the Fountains in that the first three were focused on Natalie and my life and wondering what to do about my life and loves. The second three started with my future daughter and how I am in this world with all my neurotic ideas, beliefs, and cryptic experiences. This book is a commitment to the process and fortifying my values, ideas, and ethics to develop connection and clarity.

We can see these books *are* so much about myself, and there has been a lot of thinking about what *I* want towards near giving away my entire future in different ways. This prerogative and process are how I navigate the maze and bring my work into the days where we shall assure PLU8R is a guiding and constant motive. These books are also a steady series of words and ideas for a balanced future for many, even if I sometimes don't understand I work for all.

In future Fountains, I'd like to extrapolate more about community and consect, and I'd like to focus in on some philosophy and theories about Earth and how we live. I additionally would like to target some love and truth to some people dear to me that are not just my Dad. I think the 9th Fountain book, *Sand to Silt*, shall be individually directed chapters.

My understanding of God and the Universe, and my Mom and Dad link me to write a success report to Sarah in the future. I also thank Bert, Alex, and Coleman and forming something valuable and meaningful by being Providing Point's first three patrons.

I have had negative self-worth, yet I also know I can establish a far stronger positive self-esteem and improve my work, image, and actions. I'd like to fortify the Magic codes further and think of explaining the dual lands to an audience. Not so much only the secret meanings, yet also the base mechanics and premise of how and why the Magic codes fuse. I can discuss that in *Sand to Silt* or *Nodal Input*.

It was January 24th, 2018 when a particular fool remembered a quick swim in the pool. I'm one of a specific type, though I felt a good sense of closure from the plunge with my Dad. The warmth of the air and the freshness of the water found me on the patio swimming close to this book's text.

I'm feeling thanks and relief about my process up to now. I accept I'm blessed, fortunate, and also dearly pleased and appreciative to have the life I live. I was in an exceptionally different feeling in my body, mind, and spirit when I arrived in Australia, and sadly and gladly I went home to Chilliwack

The work that I've formed up to holds merit in what it is and what it can do, though maybe it's best I don't push the Fountains. A fountain is an invitation for a drink, not a splash from a firehose! For a successful path, my stubborn nature will share them and keep forming them as they help me with my mind, being, and process.

On the chance and intuition they may be useful or hold value for another, I will keep them online with Amazon. I'm glad to have talked with Kristy this past week, and though I told her that my 20-second life story would have me hanging my head in shame. You help me write a different story.

I defiantly press on and forward because determination and perseverance are vital; I may be delusional to think that the Fountains shall be a commercial success. I shall tend more carefully to my garden back home. On the January trip, I also found that there are some that will visit the garden that allows me to let me visit theirs.

I thank you each so much. Even if you haven't yet read this, thank you for allowing me the pathways and experiences that we've had and shall have. I also commit to those who may not be able to purchase or read what I write, and for the fact that I know this planet is united and shared, my intuition reminds me to stay on course.

I heed and follow the nudges and inklings from outside of myself that tells me that even if my ethics are entirely different, some others seed grace and understanding too. I'm learning if something is a) kind, b) real, and c) helpful, we can learn to speak with purpose and direction.

The skills learned and cultivated through our years and decades may open pathways, doors, and opportunities we could never predict. If my faith in the world is correct, the abiding of higher spiritual laws and powers allows guidance, trust in myself, and my worth and understanding shall help form the sound, accurate, and actual works and value.

Right now, I'm not clear on where and what the next Fountain will do, and hadn't yet secured its completion. I let those sands drift into my mind and keys once I return home and set my feet back upon Canadian ground.

I shall get a carton of cigarettes when I'm in Hong Kong, yet the smoking is a different notion that I shan't tend to at this time. I've made changes, yet I'll clarify and share the hows and whys. I'm not clear if or how I should be writing about the past, the splayed present, or the destined future, yet the inner workings of the text shall direct the guides to remember our beautiful feathered friends in Australia.

The Contialis is an active and engaged part of our mind, and though I may believe in things that are so far out of the comprehension of others, to me, the ideas and beliefs are very legitimate. Some guess that it's a hardline fact that no one can hear our thoughts, yet I also know at night when I lay down to rest I think of how I'm reluctant to pray because humans will distort what my true self is. Corruption is a legitimate fear and concern.

The ability and practice of flowetics and rhyme are a coping mechanism and also a craft I wish to fortify and develop. Maybe those who say "no one can hear your thoughts" believe that as firmly as I do that every thought, word, decision, and movement has consequences that layer upon themselves.

I may be pushing for purpose and trying to bargain with life by promising to Providing Point instead of aiming to earn solely for myself, I may fully believe in a Natalie conspiracy, and it may be people *are* plotting my demise. I also hope now, as you read this, that the seeds have been scattered upon fertile soil and not upon the rocky shoreline.

Dare I say that my life is like a sandy island that holds brilliance and beauty and also cares for the wildlife and those who wish to visit?

My life may not be a tax as I had claimed. Instead, it may

be a sacred shroud we develop to allow lives and dreams to blossom and form. Relationships are a learned forte of mine, yet must demonstrate all the thoughts and ideas that go into forming them. Ethics and ideals are not useful unless adequately guided, manifested, and tended to.

I thank you, Dad, for allowing me the blessings, grace, and patience to be who I am, and I thank Sarah too for caring well for you and being with you in life. I pray you both more love than I'm yet aware, and Mom, I thank you for letting me be your seed of life. I may not be the fragile stone flower some presume, yet the fumed glass shall remind the tapestry that you help me by giving me good thread to sow.

The timelines and DNA I've been granted hold the fabric over the open loom to allow an unknown future to bloom and fill life with miracles. Thank you for letting us be in your garden too.

So, yeah, this is the process I committed to and follow through with as my work. The cliché of saying "It's not the destination, it's the journey" makes sense to me. I also note that if the Glass House is one of the stops along the way, I am glad to search a bit further forward to moments of forever.

It's true I could write a book all about my story, history, and past, though the Fountains are my journal and idea quarry and I'm dearly glad they form. I still think of adopting a cat again. I have a strong desire and need to love another entity, and although I can feel the pangs of grief even before we've met, there is another strong notion of hope that call me into lurching forward into the next parts of my journey.

The tree of life grows from the flows we have yet to expose, and though the rose is blue and not in the violet hue, there is a path of chalk to walk away from too. The hopes of the cosmos will speak the heart of Earth. We are not alone on this journey even if we think we are. The stars radiate through space, even at a glacial pace, to trace the fact of how my pact stacked like that tracked up upon the lawn.

Hug the people you love, and be sure to remind the dove of an infinite resolution of The Spirit is above.

ACKNOWLEDGMENTS

Thank you each who contributed to the development of our world. I am not a saviour or a prophet. The world of Earth uses me as a conduit and channel of understanding, and I am meekly thankful to know I am not alone. Even if solitary with this work, I sense spirits and energies that remind me of my wishes from more than a decade ago, and how our hearts entwine. I thank all forces of life for allowing us the grace to create, and though at a near glacial pace, I also am thankful to trace the lines of spines left along the shore that remind me some people keep us safe from the war. The premise of being aware (a-war-e) also has me grateful I need not be a soldier in a physical battle. My battles of consciousness, morality, and addiction forge these books in different ways, and through the maze reverses of curses nurse a wall called to my being. I am also thankful we see some of the fields bloom. The luxuries I've received are predominantly not understood by myself, yet creative freedom, artistic patience, and cosmic guidance are valued. I pray well that others may have such magnificent blessings for themselves too. The best that I may do at this point is to keep forging the text and revising my soul so that the shards may blend and be content to amend with every friend, lover, and entity a world of which to tend. Thank you for reading, and explicit thanks to Khans, Shards, Contialitic Guides, Sapphires, Communities and Consects, and also the Fountains Founders that allow me to do what I do. I thank you too for purchasing and reading this book and ask that you keep your beings safe, guarded, protected, nurtured, and nourished, Our Seeds germinate as we've flourished as what is wished from thee on me back to thee times three; reminding that the slogan of the Fountains Series is "From a Seed to a Tree."

Love, Light, Love, and Luck. Robert Koyich, June 23rd, 2018.

ABOUT THE AUTHOR

Rob has been working on his books since the 1st Fountain book *Finding Natalie* released in 2015. He has chosen the creative path to work for Introversial and Providing Point.

As of June 2018, the earning from Introversial's Patreon page go to Care and Share cards to support people locally. Rob relays digital versions of his books and music as additional thanks.

If you'd like to contribute to Providing Point to support people in need, please go to www.Patreon.com/Introversial.

If you'd like to hear some of Rob's music and don't want to give a monthly pledge, please go to www.KoyichDigital.Bandcamp.com. 51% of that sold through Bandcamp also go to Providing Point.

This books is the 7th Fountain and is followed by the 8th and 9th in 2018-2019. The three books will combine for the compilation *Shards of My Soul*.

The 4th, 5th, and 6th Fountains are available on Amazon individually, and also in the compilation *The Sands of Yesterday (The Second Three Fountains)*.

Journey of a Shoulsman (The First Three Fountains) was under reformation as of June 2018. It shall rerelease in September 2018.

If you'd like to contact Robert, please email:

RobertKoyich@KoyichDigital.com

Learn, Love, Live, Thrive, Create, Play, and Pray

Introversial
Providing Point
&
Koyich Digital

98498060R00064

Made in the USA
Columbia, SC
27 June 2018